Discover Gardening

with

·Dermot O'Neill·

Published 2004
Poolbeg Press Ltd.
123 Grange Hill, Baldoyle,
Dublin 13, Ireland
Email: poolbeg@poolbeg.com

A catalogue record for this book is available from the British Library.

ISBN 1-84223-184-7

Photographs by Dermot O'Neill
Designed by Steven Hope
Typeset by Patricia Hope

Printed by
Bath Press Limited • UK

www.poolbeg.com

Biography

Dermot O'Neill is one of Ireland's best-loved gardening personalities. His passion and enthusiasm for his subject touches many people and his down-to-earth, colourful, easy to follow style brings the joy of gardening to a wide audience. His keen interest in all growing things started early in childhood when Dermot's grandmother guided and encouraged him to grow plants from seed and also tend a gardening patch. These early results developed into a passion then to an all-absorbing career.

Dermot is well known for his contribution to many programmes on RTÉ, including *The Garden Show*, *Garden Heaven*, and as resident gardener on *Open House*. He is also the voice of gardening on *Today with Pat Kenny* on Radio One, makes regular contributions to *Gardeners' Corner* on BBC Radio and is the gardening correspondent for *The Sunday Times*.

Dermot has been very keenly involved with gardening and horticultural societies both at home and abroad. He is a member of twenty-eight international organisations and at home he has been a founder committee member of the Irish Garden Plants Society and a founder member of the Ranunculaceae Society. He is also a past council member of the Royal Horticultural Society of Ireland and recently he has been made a Special Friend of the Garden and Landscape Designers Association.

Dermot can be found online at **www.dermotoneill.com**, where he is delighted to receive your input and gardening queries.

Acknowledgements

I would like to thank my parents, Peter and Maura, for their fantastic support and encouragement. They are always there when I need them and their patience and guidance is greatly appreciated.

The book could not have been completed without the exceptional support of Bill O'Sullivan. A special thank you to him for his patience and help with the preparation and compilation of this book.

As with any publication, advice is sought from many sources – friends, colleagues, gardeners, experts in specialist areas and those who just have to listen to my ideas. I would like to thank them all for their time and interest in my work. I would like to acknowledge the ongoing support of Helen and Val Dillon, whose garden at 45 Sandford Road is always an inspiration. To Stephen Smith, a special word of thanks for his generosity and support. To Anna Dillon for help with proofing.

To Patricia Carroll and Michael Scott of Tyrone Productions, whose belief in my work and encouragement has made this book possible. To all of the *Open House* team, especially Marty Whelan and Mary Kennedy, Larry Masterson, Bernie O'Connor, Rosie McMeel, Dee Keane and a big thanks to Gwen Brennan.

No gardening book is the result of one person's knowledge. These are my experiences which I have amassed through so many gardening friends. Thank you to Brendan Sayers, Charlie Wilkins, John Cushnie, Brian O'Donnell and Alison Andrew.

Finally, thank you to the team at Poolbeg whose care and love of every book they publish sets them apart.

*I would like to dedicate this book to Carmel Duignan
whose wisdom, support and encouragement, particularly in
my television career, has meant so much to me*

A view of the Dillon Garden

Introduction

As a young man my gardening career was very much influenced by the people around me. One of my earliest and strongest influences was the late Barney Johnson who presented RTÉ's garden programme *The Garden*. He owned and ran what was then the country's leading garden centre – Marlfield at Cabinteely. At first, I worked there part-time and remember his encouragement and also that of Patricia King. At that time these two people had a huge influence on the career path I would take. Marlfield was a wonderful place. There I learned many things; I learned about plants and I also learned about dealing with people and realised the enjoyment I got from sharing my growing and expanding gardening knowledge with others.

From an early age I observed the generous spirit that gardeners have – the willingness to share knowledge and also the enthusiastic giving when it came to sharing plants. Through Marlfield I met a wide range of keen and influential gardeners. I recall visiting gardens which were inspiring to a young man. I have fond memories of the romantic gardens of Graigueconna near Bray, which are still lovingly cared for by Rosemary Brown. Another garden visit took me to the garden at Beech Park – a great adventure where I met its late owner David Shackleton and saw within its walled garden one of the greatest plant collections in these isles. In those days there were not so many gardens open to the public. Of course, there were Powerscourt and Mount Usher, which ranked among the great gardens, but it was the many private gardens which held a deep fascination. These gardens were often created by plant enthusiasts and, at that time, I was keen to learn as much as possible. Through these enthusiasts and their gardens I was introduced constantly to new plants. I remember being told that one of the best ways to learn about a plant is to grow that plant. My own garden then was limited in terms of space, as were my funds, so the next best thing was to share the knowledge of plants with gardeners who grew them.

There was always a great sense of excitement when you were invited to visit a private garden – a sense of being admitted to the inner sanctum. This was especially exciting when the garden you were going to visit was noted for its plant collection or the owner had a reputation for growing a particular plant rather well.

A regular invitation came from the Ms Charlton's. These two ladies lived in Howth and gardened on many terraces on the side of the hill. They drew water from their own well and their afternoon tea and baking was never to be forgotten. This terraced garden was full of old-fashioned favourites and overflowed with atmosphere. Their speciality was growing old varieties of primulas including wonderful double types and the then rare and choice double-flowered auriculas. They grew many from seed and it was always a treat in spring to visit and see the latest seedlings flower. I remember the rich, sweet fragrance of these primulas and being fascinated by their double auriculas, which were in colours of lemon yellow, chartreuse green and blue-tinged French grey. They also grew gold-laced primulas. In the days when I visited, these plants were exceptionally difficult to find. They were the kind of plant that were usually passed or swapped from one gardener to another. The thought of finding them in garden centres then was like finding a hen with teeth. I had always loved these plants as I had good memories of them from my grandmother's garden. It was wonderful to exchange growing tips and to find out how to get the best from these plants. The Charlton's were expert growers and one left not only with added knowledge but usually with a bag full of freshly-dug plants for one's own garden. Their enthusiasm and generosity of spirit I was to find in many gardens around the country.

This spirit I also discovered by joining many gardening clubs and societies over the years. There are gardening clubs all over the country and becoming a member of one of these is a great way to meet like-minded people, a great way to share, and a great way to nurture your interest while you nurture that interest in others. Early on, the Royal Horticultural Society of Ireland played an important role for me. Being a member opened a forum for discussion and many gardening friends were made, which I still have today.

Having a deep love of growing things has, over the years, made me look closely at different plant groups that are collected and grown, often by specialists, for example orchids, cacti and succulents, bonsai, insectivorous plants and alpines. By talking to experts, and especially those who have devoted themselves to a particular group of plants, I have been able to get great insights and shared wisdoms which have contributed to my knowledge of growing plants in general. My knowledge of growing plants comes from a great pool of shared expertise. In this book, I have selected many of these special plant areas and share with you a distillation of the growing techniques. These are needed to succeed with what are often a very simple and easy group of

plants to grow, if one follows the basic rules. One thing I have learned is that by growing a plant, be it simply from seed or taking a cutting, by nurturing and caring for that plant, you share in a collective experience – the experience of gardening. You don't have to have specialist knowledge. You don't have to have great expertise. All you have to have is a willingness to try and to learn from your mistakes. We've all killed plants and in that process we learn something. We learn by our mistakes. To grow a plant to perfection most definitely means that we have made mistakes somewhere along the line and we have learned from those. So to participate in the joy of gardening, don't be afraid, have a go, and learn as you go.

Contents

Annuals & Biennials   1

Sowing Seeds Outdoors   8

Hanging Baskets & Window Boxes   13

Bonsai   17

Orchids   25

Carnivorous Plants   33

Rock Garden & Alpine Plants   39

Herbs   47

Cactl & Other Succulents   55

Soft Fruit - Strawberries & Raspberries   65

Ornamental Grasses   73

Hedges   77

Topiary   83

Propagation   89

Tree Fruit   95

Conservatory Plants   103

Scented Plants   109

Weeds & Weed Control   113

Annuals & Biennials

Annuals

An annual is a plant raised from seed in the same year for a summer or autumn display. It is a plant which flowers and dies in a single season. Annuals grown from seed are usually divided into two categories:

• Half-hardy annuals are those which are sensitive to frost and will need to be started off under protection.

• Hardy annuals are raised from seed for a spring, summer or autumn display. When sown in spring, they will flower and die in a single season. For an early-flowering display, an outdoor sowing can be made the previous September. This will provide an earlier display the following year.

Buying

Half-hardy annuals are often referred to as bedding plants. They are usually on sale in garden centres around the country before it is safe to plant them out. If you buy them early it may be necessary to put them in a coldframe or to cover them at night until all risk of frost has gone. When buying bedding plants from a garden centre always make sure that the plants are bushy and, if possible, avoid those in full flower.

Planting Out

When planting out, sprinkle a dressing of general fertiliser and lightly rake this into the soil. Water the tray a few hours before planting. Use a trowel and group your plants, positioning them between 6 and 12in apart. Be careful to position taller-growing varieties behind the shorter ones and give some thought to colour combining, either harmonising or contrasting colours. Water plants in well afterwards and it will be necessary to water for several weeks on a regular basis until the new plants become well established.

Pests

After planting, it is important to keep an eye out for greenfly as these can often cluster on new shoots. It will be necessary to treat accordingly.

Biennials

A biennial is a plant raised from seed for a spring or early summer display. The first season, it will produce stems and leaves. In the second season it will flower. After flowering, biennial plants die. There are many garden plants we treat as biennials, for example foxgloves, wallflowers and sweet william. These are actually short-lived perennials, but for garden display purposes they are often best treated as biennials. The seed for these is best sown outdoors in May or June. I usually isolate a small part of the vegetable garden for this. By the end of September they are moved to the flowering position.

Sowing

The majority of biennials should be sown in early summer, but I suggest you leave stocks, forget-me-nots and evening primrose until mid-summer. When the plants are large enough they can be lifted and replanted into the garden for flowering the following spring. It is important not to plant them too late as this will not give them sufficient time to develop a proper root system before the soil and weather become too cold. Biennials require well-drained soil. They are easily planted using a trowel. Firm the soil around the roots as it may have been loosened when they were dug up. If the weather in autumn is dry it will be necessary to water them into position. At this stage, it is a good idea to pinch the tips of wallflower to encourage flowering shoots.

Buying

If you don't have time to grow your own annuals and biennials from seed, they are always available in garden centres. Seasonal varieties will be available for spring, summer and autumn planting.

Annuals

Ageratum
Height: 6in
Spread: 6in
Rounded pink or blue flowerheads.
Sun

Calendula (Pot Marigold)
Height: 12in
Spread: 9in
Orange, yellow or cream flowers.
Sun

Centaurea (Cornflower)
Height: 2ft
Spread: 12in
Available in many colours. Most popular in blue.
Sun or light shade

Cosmos
Height: Up to 3ft
Spread: 12in
Single, small dahlia-like flowers in pink, white or red.
Needs sun

Lathyrus (Sweet Pea)
Height: 3 to 8ft
Spread: 6 to 8in
Wide range of colours. Often powerfully scented.
Sun

Calendula (Pot Marigold)

Centaurea (Cornflower)

Lathyrus (Sweet Pea)

Lobelia erinus
Height: 6in
Spread: 4in
Also available in trailing varieties. Blue, red, pink or white flowers. Long flowering period.
Sun or light shade

Matthiola bicornis (Night-scented Stock)
Height: 12in
Spread: 9in
Strongly scented, pale lilac coloured flowers.
Sun

Nicotiana (Tobacco Plant)
Height: 1 to 3ft
Spread: 1ft
Mixed colours. Often evening scented.
Sun

Petunia
Height: 9 to 12in
Spread: 9 to 12in
Trumpet shaped flowers in a wide range of bright colours.
Sun

Tagetes (French Marigold)
Height: 6in
Spread: 6in
Round flowers of yellow-orange or gold. French marigolds are compact, often with bi-coloured flowers.
Sun

Lobelia erinus 'Crystal Palace'

Petunia

Tagetes (French Marigold)

Verbena

Tropaeolum (Nasturtium)
Height: 12in
Spread: 12in
Red, orange or yellow.
Sun or shade

Verbena
Height: 6 to 12in
Spread: 6 to 12in
Various colours including red, purple, pink
and white.
Sun

Note: *Average height and spread are given, but
these may vary with different varieties.*

Lupins - Mixed hybrids

Biennials

Bellis perennis (Batchelor's Button)
Height: 5in
Spread: 5in
White or pink.
Sun or shade

Campanula medium (Canterbury Bell)
Height: 30in
Spread: 12in
Bell-shaped flowers in white, pink or blue.
Sun

Cheiranthus (Wallflower)
Height: 12 to 18in
Spread: 12in
Wide range of different varieties available, coming in an almost full spectrum of colour, often with a rich scent.
Sun

Dianthus barbatus (Sweet William)
Height: 18in
Spread: 9in
Mixed colours available.
Sun

Digitalis (Foxglove)
Height: 4ft
Spread: 15in
Tall and dwarf varieties are available and they come in pastel shades including white and spotted types.
Shade

Cheiranthus (Wallflower)

Dianthus barbatus (Sweet William)

Matthiola incana (Brompton Stock)

Lunaria (Honesty)
Height: 2ft
Spread: 9in
Mauve, pink or white flowers followed by silver penny-shaped seedpots.
Light shade

Matthiola incana (Brompton Stock)
Height: 18in
Spread: 9in
White, pink or mauve. Double or single clustered flowers. Sweetly scented.
Sun

Myosotis (Forget-me-not)
Height: 9in
Spread: 6in
Usually blue, but there are also pink and white varieties available.
Sun or shade

Oenothera biennis (Evening Primrose)
Height: 2ft
Spread: 12in
Saucer-shaped yellow flowers.
Sun

Papaver nudicaule (Iceland Poppy)
Height: 30in
Spread: 9in
Tissue paper orange, yellow and pink flowers.
Sun

Note: *Average height and spread are given, but these may vary with different varieties.*

Digitalis (Foxglove)

Papaver nudicaule (Iceland Poppy)

Sowing Seeds Outdoors

– Six Easy Steps to Success

1. Select the Right Time

Hardy biennials are sown from early May until the end of July. June is an ideal month for this job. Hardy annuals are best sown in March or April, but keep an eye on weather conditions as it is important that the soil is warm enough to allow germination and also dry enough for you to work the soil, making a good seedbed. There are also quite a few hardy annuals, for example cornflower and gypsophila, which can be sown directly in September. If you decide to make an autumn sowing of these annuals you can expect them to flower earlier than the spring sowings.

2. Prepare the Seed-sowing Bed

Select an open position away from overhanging trees and shrubs. Lightly fork over the soil and add some soil conditioner, but avoid fertiliser at this stage. Lightly tread over the bed with your heels and then rake the soil to provide an even surface.

3. Drills

Drills should be 6 to 12in apart. Make them deep enough to allow the seed to be covered with soil to about twice the size of the seed. Do NOT water the bed after sowing. If the soil is dry you can lightly water it before you sow.

4. Sowing

Always sow seed thinly and avoid sowing directly from the packet. I always recommend that you place some seed in the palm of your hand and gently sprinkle using your thumb and finger. After sowing, lightly rake the soil back into the drill, firming the soil with the back of the rake. Again, do not water. Some seeds will need to be protected from birds. Horticultural fleece can help with this.

5. Thinning Out

After the first true leaves have developed on your seedlings you are ready to thin. Remove excess seedlings, leaving one seedling every 2in. It is important not to disturb the seedlings you wish to hold on to. Two weeks later, repeat the process, this time spacing 4in apart. Larger-growing plants may need more room of up to a 6in interval.

6. Planting Out

Using a trowel, lift biennials in autumn and transfer to the flowerbeds where you want them to bloom. Autumn sown hardy annuals can be planted into their permanent position in April or May.

Salpiglossis 'Chocolate Pot'

Hints

Mulching Windowboxes
One problem with windowboxes is that wet soil can often splash onto windowpanes. This often happens during heavy rain, especially when newly planted. To help prevent this, a top covering of gravel around the plants prevents soil splashing.

Planting Up Hanging Baskets
When filling a hanging basket, it is a good idea to plant from the inside out. Push plants through the sides after positioning their roots carefully from within.

Watering Hanging Baskets
To help save time and energy when watering hanging baskets, especially those positioned up high, it is a good idea to fix a bamboo cane along the last few feet of your hose. This will keep the hose rigid and help you to reach the higher baskets more easily.

Sowing Tiny Seeds
When sowing tiny seeds it is a good idea to mix them with some dry sand. Sprinkle this evenly. The pale colour of the sand will show up against the dark soil and the tiny seed will be more evenly distributed.

Pinching Out
Pinch out the tops of annuals and some biennial plants, especially those that tend to grow long and spindly. Use your thumb and forefinger to remove the growing tip. This encourages bushiness and works extremely well on plants such as Solenostemon (Coleus) and wallflowers. This will encourage sideshoots to develop quickly and give the whole plant a more attractive overall shape.

Deadheading
Some of the most popular winter-flowering bedding plants are pansies, which come in a wide range of colours. To guarantee as long a flowering season as possible it is important to remove the dead flowers. By doing this you are encouraging the plant's energy to go into providing new flowers rather than setting seed from the old.

Care Calendar

January

Sow half-hardy annuals under glass.

February

Begin sowing annual climbers. Continue early sowing of slow-maturing bedding and half-hardy annuals.

March

Complete sowing of annual climbers. Prick out seedlings of earlier sowings as soon as they produce their first true leaves. Sow hardy annuals in a cold frame or unheated greenhouse.

April

Begin to harden off young plants. Start to sow hardy annuals directly into flowering position.

May

Transplant overwintered annuals into their final flowering positions. Clear spring bedding plants. In mild areas, plant out hardened-off annuals when the danger of frost has passed.

June

Sow fast-maturing summer annuals. Sow spring-flowering biennials.

July

Deadhead to encourage repeat flowering. Continue to sow biennials.

August

Pinch out tips of wallflowers. Collect and store seed.

September

Sow annuals to overwinter. Plant out spring-flowering annuals and biennials in flowering positions to give plants time to establish before winter.

October

Complete planting of spring-flowering annuals and biennials.

November

Cover hardy annuals with horticultural fleece during bad weather.

December

Get new season seed catalogues and place orders for the coming season.

Hanging Baskets & Window Boxes

Hanging baskets add a splash of colour to any garden, but they can also add height and scale to outdoor planting. They are ideal for gardens where space is limited. Hanging baskets are most often used for summer bedding plants, but in recent years people are also using them for winter displays where winter pansies, primulas, ivies and other evergreens really come into their own.

The wire hanging basket is the traditional basket for summer and often winter displays. These have traditionally been lined with a thick layer of moss to help conserve moisture and support the compost. Moss is no longer as freely available as it has been in the past so you may like to choose from some of the ready-made liners available in garden centres today. Although many of these are practical and convenient, they may not have the charm of natural moss.

Five Steps to Making Your Own Hanging Basket

1. Line the basket up to about a third of the way up the sides with a good layer of moss. Then fill with compost to the top of the lining. Firm gently.

2. Arrange the first row of plants gently, teasing the foliage through the holes in the basket from the inside out to avoid having to crush the roots of the plants.

3. When the first row of plants are in place, add more moss (if you are lining with moss) to the basket to two thirds of the way up. Then add compost to the same level, firming gently around the plants.

4.   Arrange the second row of plants in the same way as the first, placing them in the spaces between the first plants. Line to the top with moss and then fill with compost.

5.   Plant the rest of the plants in the top of the basket, arranging the outer ones at a slight angle to encourage them to tumble over the side of the basket. Water thoroughly.

Watering

In very warm weather, hanging baskets may need to be watered twice daily. There are ways that you can cut down on this:

• Line the basket with plastic inside the moss lining. This helps to reduce moisture loss. One or two drainage holes will be necessary

• Improve the water retaining ability of the compost you use by adding a good handful of organic matter such as well-rotted manure. An alternative to this is to use moisture retaining crystals which store water and gradually release it into the compost.

• Place a saucer in the bottom of the basket before adding the compost. This will act as a reservoir, storing water.

Feeding

As the hanging basket is constantly being watered throughout the growing season, it will be necessary to replace nutrients. A liquid feed used at slightly weaker than the recommended dose on a regular basis will help to keep your basket in top condition. When in full flower, a liquid tomato feed is ideal for helping to sustain colour. Always make sure that the basket is moist before applying a liquid feed. If a basket becomes too dry it may be necessary to lift it, placing it in a basin of water where it can gradually absorb water again. This should be done in advance of using any liquid feeding.

Windowboxes

When planting with summer or winter colour you can create a matching colour scheme with both windowbox and hanging basket. This helps to create unity in your display. Always make sure that windowboxes are firmly secured. The extra weight of plants as they develop and a possible lack of water can cause them to tumble off a windowledge, possibly causing severe damage or injury. Also, with hanging baskets, make sure that the bracket is not only secured well but is of correct strength for the size of basket, remembering that when it is fully watered it can be very heavy.

Chamaecyparis obtrusa

Bonsai

The Oriental art of bonsai is a fascinating one. Originating in China and later developed and perfected in Japan, these miniature trees capture everybody's imagination when they see them. This art involves the pruning of a tree or a shrub in such a way as to restrict its growth and to keep it as a miniature version of its true self. A very important aspect is the shallow dish or container in which it is grown, the idea being to make the plant look as though it is part of a miniature landscape. The technique involved in maintaining a bonsai is a combination of nature and art. Growing one or creating a collection allows you to create a natural world in miniature.

Creating your own bonsai is easy and can be a very inexpensive form of gardening, especially if you are creating your own from scratch. Great cost can be involved when you purchase an already created piece of living art. In Japan many of these special miniature trees are handed down from generation to generation and are venerated as a direct link with the ancestors who created them. Anyone can acquire the skill to create their own bonsai. Very little space is required. The techniques which are used are closely related to those of full-scale gardening. To start, all that is required is an appreciation of nature.

Crataegus oxycantha

Creating a Bonsai

When creating a bonsai, the aim is to make a perfect miniature tree or shrub, displaying it on its own or with others in a landscape. Bonsai are not grown usually in pots but in shallow dishes. This not only restricts their root growth but also provides a large surface area on which you can arrange stones, small pieces of rock and moss to create a setting. Tradition has dictated that the older, more gnarled-looking the plant, the better. This means that a plant needs to be pruned and wired to produce the impression of an aged, often windswept tree.

Selecting a Tree

Virtually any tree or shrub can be used, but it is best to choose plants which have naturally small leaves as these will help to retain a sense of scale. Fast-growing trees will need regular attention but quickly form interesting bonsai. Slower-growing plants and trees need far less pruning but take much longer to make a mature specimen. Conifers such as pines are evergreen with year-round foliage. These add an extra decorative touch to a collection in winter. Many deciduous trees produce beautiful autumn colour and the tracery of their branches provides attractive winter interest. Many flowering shrubs and trees can be used such as azaleas, wisteria and *crataegus* (hawthorn). Berrying plants like cotoneaster can add to a collection.

Making a Start

There are two ways of creating your own bonsai. One which probably gives you the most control is to grow a plant from a seed or cutting. This way you can shape it as it grows. The other way, especially useful if you are a beginner or feel you don't quite have the patience to start from seed, is to get going with an existing young plant which you can buy from a garden centre or specialist outlet. Pruning and wiring the tree to the shape you want will help

you to learn basic techniques quickly. First you will need to remove the plant from its pot, shake off the soil and follow these steps:

1. Remove any tangles that have resulted from the plant being pot-bound. Carefully rake out the roots working outwards from the trunk. Next trim back any long roots.

2. Remove any loose roots severed while raking out and any with a strong tendency to grow downwards. Next, reduce the mass of roots by cutting out up to four triangular pieces.

3. Cut out any dead or damaged foliage and stems. Trim back close to the trunk any main branches growing in the wrong direction or crossing each other.

For the beginner this may seem like rather drastic measures, but it is necessary to achieve the miniature result that will make your first bonsai.

Shaping

It is a good idea to rotate the tree while you are working on it. This way you will be able to view it from all sides so you can judge the best shape. It is also a good idea to stand back from the tree and to walk around it from time to time so that you can evaluate the shape as it develops.

1. To start with, you will need a pair of sharp cutters. There are special cutters available which can be obtained via the internet or from a specialist outlet. Begin to shape the plant by removing any of the branches which spoil the appearance, but always remember that these changes are permanent so take your time and consider each cut with care.

2. It is not unusual that you will need to wire the branches temporarily. This will help to pull them down into a more desirable position. Use a thick copper wire for the lower branches and a thinner wire for the upper ones.

3. Wrap the wire around the trunk and then the branches. Leave it in place for up to six months, then cut it off. It's important to keep a watchful eye on the wire, removing it earlier if it starts to cut into the bark. The tree may need to be wired again for a second time if the branches revert to their original positions.

4. When the branches are in the correct position, stand back and take a look at the overall appearance. At this stage, it may be necessary to remove shoots on the underside of the branches. These can easily be snipped off if they are small and in some cases they can even be pinched off with your fingertips.

Potting

Choose a potting compost that is well drained and yet has moisture-retentive properties. Your finished and now shaped tree should be planted in a traditional container where it will stay for up to two years before it will need repotting. The traditional containers are usually shallow. Terracotta or ceramic look far better than plastic, giving you a more authentic look. Correct placement of your tree in the container is important, always keeping balance and harmony in mind.

Juniperus chinensis

Care

If you are buying an existing bonsai, it is important to check on purchase whether it is an indoor or outdoor tree. Some types are tender and will not survive outside, whereas the opposite applies to outdoor trees which will not cope with indoor conditions. The best place for growing the majority of outdoor bonsai is in a sheltered bright spot out of direct sunlight. Remember, owning a bonsai is like owning a pet – they are a responsibility and need constant care and attention. Watering is needed every day except in winter. Feeding is often required depending on the size, age and type of tree. When your tree becomes pot-bound it will need to be moved correctly to the next sized container. At this stage, root pruning may be necessary. Bonsai need constant and regular attention when it comes to developing the tree's full potential and shape.

Hints

Compost

Give your indoor bonsai the best soil or compost mix you can buy.

Pot

Make sure you choose the correct pot. The pot is to a bonsai what a frame is to a painting. The wrong pot will not enhance your tree in the same way a badly-framed watercolour loses its charm.

Indoor or Outdoor?

Remember to check when buying your bonsai whether it is an indoor or outdoor type as care will differ accordingly.

Tools

Specialist bonsai outlets or specialist bonsai nurseries on the internet offer a range of tools which have been specially adapted and developed for the special cultural requirements of the plants. These make a good investment. The rule is you get what you pay for.

Watering

Remember that the quality of water you use will affect the overall health of your bonsai. The ideal is rainwater as this is soft and gentle to the plant.

Misting

In winter, indoor bonsai will require regular misting to counterbalance the dry atmosphere, especially where there is central heating.

Acer palmatum

Bonsai Babysitter

If you plan holidays for extended periods, it may be necessary to train a bonsai babysitter in advance.

Cascading Bonsai

Psycopsis papilo (Oncidium papilo)

Orchids

Gardeners have always regarded orchids as exotic, expensive and difficult to grow. This is a reputation they inherited from the days of the big house when there were special greenhouses and gardeners to care for these fabulous plants as they were first being discovered and introduced. Today, orchids are widely available, are most definitely affordable and many can be grown on the kitchen windowsill. The secret to success is understanding their simple requirements and choosing the correct types.

Orchid

Care

Orchids are divided into three groups of care. These groups are known as the cool house, the intermediate house and the warm house. Orchids that belong to the cool house and many from the intermediate can easily be grown without providing extra special conditions. These groups refer to the temperature at which different orchids are happiest growing in. Temperature is one of the most important factors when considering developing a collection. Cool house orchids are among the easiest to grow requiring a temperature no lower than 50 degrees farenheit. These include *Dendrobium* and *Cymbidium*. Intermediate is where the temperature is not allowed to drop below 55 degrees. Orchids like *Miltonia* and *Paphiopedilum* fall into this category. And the warm house varieties requires a minimum night temperature of at least 65 degrees, but the temperature should not exceed 80 degrees farenheit. With this group of orchids it is necessary to have high humidity. Orchids which fall into this category include *Vanda* and *Phalaenopsis*.

Watering

To understand how orchids grow in the wild gives great insight into their watering and potting requirements. In nature many of the exotic orchids we grow in our homes grow clinging to branches high up in the canopy of trees in the rainforest. Here their roots are restricted and they are exposed to regular wettings from rainforest conditions. So in your own home watering is required on a regular basis while allowing the plants to dry for short periods in between, mimicking what would happen in a rainforest. Wetting by rain, getting dry and getting wet again is the general idea. Your orchids should never be stood in water. They will also enjoy humidity which is alien to our homes so an occasional light misting and even standing them on a gravel tray which contains a reservoir of water can assist in providing the extra moisture in the air around the plants. Generally orchids prefer to be pot-bound and often when you purchase a plant it seems to be bursting from the pot. This is natural and repotting should only be carried out as the centre of the plant becomes old and the outer parts require fresh root space.

If you become an enthusiastic collector of orchids you will discover that there are hundreds if not more available through specialist nurseries. There are organisations and societies devoted to the subject which can help expand your knowledge and insight into the special care some of the more unusual species and types require.

Cattleya

This orchid is best known as the corsage orchid. They are very adaptable and certainly provide extraordinarily exotic blooms. Many have a beautiful rich fragrance. Flowers are available in a wide range of colours and sizes.

Light: As with other orchids, Cattleyas prefer an east or lightly-shaded south facing windowsill.

Temperature: Provide a night-time temperature of 55 to 60 degrees and a daytime temperature of 70 to 90 degrees farenheit.

Watering: They should be watered once or twice a week. They may be allowed to dry out between watering.

Cattleya hybrid

Cymbidium

Cymbidiums are one of the most widely available and popular orchids for winter and spring flowering. The beautiful sprays of flowers, if purchased when the first flowerbuds open, will remain in bloom for many months. Cybidiums are one of the easiest and most rewarding of orchids to grow, ideal for the beginner.

Light: Place Cymbidiums in a bright spot out of direct sunlight. Too much light and the leaves will yellow. Insufficient light will cause the leaves to turn dark green.

Cymbididium lowianum

Temperature*:* Mature plants require a night-time temperature of below 60 degrees farenheit during early autumn. This helps to initiate flowering. For best results, provide night-time temperatures of 50 to 60 degrees farenheit and daytime temperatures of 70 to 85 degrees farenheit.

Watering: Depending on temperature Cymbidiums should be watered about once or twice a week. The rule of thumb for watering should be more heat more water, less heat less water. Cymbidiums prefer to be kept on the moist side, but this does not mean that they like to be left standing in water.

Dendrobium

Dendrobium is an excellent choice for anyone starting to grow orchids for the first time. There is

a wide range of colours available in different sizes and shapes. If you purchase a plant in bud, you can expect to have the plant flowering for up to two months.

Light*:* The best position for this orchid is on an east-facing windowsill or a lightly-shaded south-facing windowledge.

Temperature: Provide night-time temperatures of 55 to 60 degrees farenheit and daytime 70 to 90 degrees farenheit.

Watering: Depending on the temperature they should be watered once or twice a week. Dendrobiums must be allowed to dry out completely in between watering. When watering, try to do it early in the day so that they are dry by nightfall.

Oncidium

These plants can be grown with great ease in the home. They are popular for their striking sprays of flowers and flexibility in growing conditions.

Light: They thrive in bright light out of direct sunlight. They can be put outside during summer in a sheltered spot, protected from strong sunlight.

Temperature: For best results, provide a night-time temperature of 60 degrees farenheit and a daytime temperature of under 85 degrees farenheit.

Watering: Should be watered about two or three times a week. These orchids prefer to be kept on the moist side.

Phalaenopsis

One of the most widely available of orchids today, commonly seen in florist shops, these plants adapt very well to home conditions. From the time first buds open you can expect Phalaenopsis to remain in flower for up to three months.

Light: Provide a bright position out of direct sunlight. An east-facing window is ideal. If exposed to too much sunlight the foliage may burn.

Dendrobium hybrid

Temperature: Normal household temperatures are ideal (between 75 and 85 degrees farenheit).

Watering: Every four to five days. This orchid likes to be kept on the moist side but, again, avoid standing the plant in water.

Odontoglossum hybrid

Care Calendar

Odontocidium hybrid

January

During winter months artificial heating is necessary in greenhouses. For Cymbidium night-time temperature should not be allowed to fall below 54 degrees farenheit. White-flowered species of Cymbidium are more fragile than others.

February

When watering, avoid wetting the centre of the plant. Plants mounted on bark can be given more water, except for Dendrobiums which are still resting. Dendrobiums should be just given enough water to stop the plant becoming wrinkled.

March

Watch out for emerging flower spikes, marking their presence with a short bamboo cane. This may help to prevent them getting broken. Cattleyas which flowered in the autumn should be repotted now if necessary.

April

Keep an eye out for pests. Repot any plants which need it as soon as they have finished flowering. Cymbidium should be watered every fortnight with a liquid orchid fertiliser. Important tasks this month are repotting and cleaning along with watering.

May

Keep an eye out for botrytis (fungal attack) and treat accordingly. During this month some orchids may be sensitive to excessive heat but must not be exposed to any chill.

June

Many orchids can be moved to an outdoor position in summer. Position them where they will receive early morning or late afternoon sun. Provide shade during the hottest part of the day. Give full attention to ventilation and watering.

July

Check that small plants are not blown over by wind. Watering and damping down are very important tasks this month. Rainwater is recommended. Orchids will cope with excessive high temperatures better if the humidity is also high to balance it.

August

Continue damping down in between pots.

September

Slugs and red spider mite may remain a problem this month. As temperatures start to cool, plants placed outdoors should be brought back indoors.

Odontocidium hybrid

October

Where leaves have turned yellow either allow them to drop off naturally or cut them off with a sterilised tool. Continue to water in moderation.

November

Check heating carefully. Renew the plastic covering on the inside of the greenhouse and clean the glass to admit as much light as possible. Stop damping down the plants. Make sure your plants are not standing too close to the glass or window where the cold could harm them.

December

Artificial heating may be in constant use which dries the air inside. Treat the lack of humidity by spraying the ground or greenhouse floor. Cold water must not be used on orchids in winter.

Odontocidium hybrid

Dionaea muscipula

Carnivorous Plants

Carnivorous plants are among some of the most awe-inspiring and intriguing plants on the planet. Many have an exotic appearance. The best-known is possibly the Venus Fly Trap, but this is only one of a large range of fascinating and easy-to-grow plants. These plants have evolved to seek their food from other sources apart from the soil. The soil they grow in is usually extremely poor with little or no nutrients. Nature has assisted them by evolving a sophisticated method whereby the plants have adapted themselves to trap insects which they digest to find nourishment.

Dionaea muscipula 'Venus Fly Trap'

Venus Fly Trap (*Dionaea*)

Venus Fly Traps can only be found naturally in North and South Carolina in the USA. The plant forms small rosettes of approximately six to eight leaves. The leaf is the trap. On the inside surface of the trap are several tiny hairs. These are the triggers. For the trap to close, these hairs must be stimulated several times within twenty seconds. If an insect, for example a fly, disturbs these hairs the two lobes making up the leaf will quickly close and the whole process of digesting the fly begins.

Sundew (*Drosera*)

Sundews exist all over the world. There are even Irish natives. Most enjoy growing in bog-like conditions. They are among the easiest of the carnivorous plants to grow. Sundews produce a very sticky liquid on the ends of mobile tentacles which are gathered on the upper surface of its leaves. Insects which lodge on these tentacles are trapped by the sticky liquid. The tentacles slowly move the insect to the centre of the leaf where digestion starts. In some species the whole leaf will fold or curl around the insect, holding it in place with its sticky grip.

Cobra Lily (*Darlingtonia*)

The Darlingtonia is commonly known as the Cobra Lily due to its sinister cobra-like stance. It grows in the mountains of California and Oregon. Insects are attracted and tempted inside. Once inside, they find it difficult to find their way through the small opening back to the outside world. The inside of the tube contains a liquid and eventually the insect

Nepenthes

Darlingtonia californica

drowns in this. Bacteria come into play and before long the Cobra Lily has turned its insect victims into soup.

Nepenthes

Nepenthes certainly rank among nature's greatest curiosities and in the world of carnivorous plants these have to be the most exotic and fearsome looking. Upturned pitchers grow from the ends of their leaves. Some are brightly coloured. In nature these plants grow in extremely poor soil so it is necessary for them to attract insects which they assimilate using special digestive glands and enzymes for dissolving their prey. Nepenthes are not widely available and are probably the most demanding to grow.

Sarracenia (Pitcher Plant)

Pitcher Plant (*Sarracenia*)

The Pitcher Plant attracts, catches and digests insects. They are natives of south-eastern USA and Canada. They grow in a range of shapes and sizes, ranging from small, squat plants to tall, elegant, elongated plants. They flower usually from the end of April until early July, individual flowers usually lasting for about three weeks. The flower colour varies from white through to yellow, orange and even deep red. Many hybrids have been developed with quite spectacular flowers of varying shades.

Pitcher Plant (Flower)

Care Calendar

Sarracenia, Dionacea and Drosera all require a period of dormancy in winter. This means that the plant needs cooler conditions between October and January, until the plant starts to regrow in spring. At this time it is best to reduce watering so that conditions are just damp.

Darlingtonia must have cool conditions and good humidity. It also likes a long, cold-weather dormancy in winter. It is best grown in live sphagnum moss. It is a difficult plant to grow in anything but chilly areas. Cold growing conditions are the secret of success.

Remove or cut off any dead leaves or traps. In the case of pitcher plants and Darlingtonia it is best to cut off the browning leaf tops as they die back, keeping the green parts intact. When the leaves are completely dead carefully remove them from the rhizome or crown.

Drosera 'Sundew'

Growing Instructions

Carnivorous plants are not difficult to grow. They make a wonderful if somewhat bizarre-looking collection when grouped together. They always fascinate, especially the young. The care is very straightforward providing you follow a few simple rules.

Position in full sunlight. They are best in an unheated greenhouse or conservatory or are also suitable for a south-facing windowsill.

Avoid   using tapwater. Collected rainwater or distilled water is best.

Never   allow your plant to dry out.

Avoid   giving any liquid feed.

Repot   every three years in a mixture of moss peat and perlite. Do not use potting compost and avoid lime.

Hints

No flies?

If your plant does not have access to flies, you will need to catch insects, for example woodlice. It is best to use live insects as these stimulate the plant to start the digestive process.

Compost

For pitcher plants and Darlingtonia, 6 parts peat (not compost), 3 parts perlite or vermiculite, 1 part coarse sand. For Venus Fly Traps and Sundews 3 parts peat, 1 part coarse sand.

Sarracenia (Pitcher Plant)

Greenfly

Although carnivorous plants eat insects many can suffer from greenfly attack. These congregate on the soft new growth. Small infestations can be wiped off with a finger.

Venus Fly Trap

It is important not to over-stimulate the traps on a venus fly trap. After closing two or possibly three times the trap becomes exhausted and dies. This can often weaken and kill a plant.

Liquid Feeding?

The root system on carnivorous plants has not evolved to take in food so liquid feed can easily kill them.

Watering

Tap water contains flouride and, in some areas, there are high levels of lime which carnivorous plants do not like. It is best to use rainwater which has been collected.

Rock Garden & Alpine Plants

Yellow Rock Rose in trough

Alpine and rock garden plants have great appeal. If you are a gardener with only limited space, these plants make it possible to grow a wide range. They are also very suitable for growing in raised beds which is ideal for anyone suffering from back trouble or those working from a wheelchair. There is a huge range to choose from.

Alpine and rock garden plants can be grown in a wide range of situations. You could make a rock garden which is ideal for setting off and displaying these small plants. They're also very suitable for growing in old-fashioned stone troughs, and raised beds are ideal too because of the extra drainage they provide, which is essential to the success of these plants.

Alpine and rock garden plants appreciate being planted close to rocks. The rocks will provide warmth and a moist, cool root-run during the warm summer months. In winter the rocks will also provide some protection from bad weather. During very warm weather rocks will help plants survive by trapping some moisture underneath.

Alpine and rock garden plants can suffer more from winter wet than the excesses of cold during winter. A pane of glass anchored with a stone will help to keep wet away from the centre or crown of plants. It is important that air can circulate freely when the glass is in place.

It is essential for your plants to have good drainage. Extra drainage material can be added if you are constructing an area from scratch. Otherwise planting your plants in crevices or making small raised areas that can be filled with free-draining compost will help.

Alpine Troughs & Containers

Small rock garden plants are ideal for troughs, tubs and old Belfast sinks. They will need a well-drained compost with extra grit added. The use of cleverly positioned rocks with a top-dressing of light gravel will help to create a miniature landscape. Make sure to position the trough before you start work as it may become excessively heavy to move later.

Many alpines and rock garden plants make ideal subjects for planting in pots or shallow pans. This is an ideal way for growing some of the more difficult types. You have greater control over compost, watering and feeding and as the plants are portable it allows you to overwinter them in the protection of a cold greenhouse. Make sure that the containers have sufficient drainage in the base and top-dress the surface of the pot, including beneath the crown of the plant, with light gravel or grit. This helps to keep the top of the plant from rotting.

Buying

Garden centres offer an extensive range of alpine plants. These are available year-round, but as many are spring flowering you will often find the best selection available then. However, it is a good idea to buy flowering plants in each season to help extend colour in the rock garden throughout the year. When buying always select plants that look healthy and make sure that the pots are free from weeds, as you do not want to add what may be a pernicious weed to your garden. Also, try to avoid plants which are obviously pot-bound. This is easy to recognise as the roots will be coming through the bottom of the pot in excess.

Gentian acaulis

This is a classic rock garden plant and certainly ranks as one of the essentials. It is generally easy to grow but can be shy to flower. Beautiful deep gentian blue flowers appear in late spring and then again sometimes in autumn. Height: 3in, Spread: 1ft.

Gentian acaulis

Pulsatilla vulgaris

Commonly called the pasque flower with lovely trumpet bell-shaped flowers in spring followed by silky seedheads. Comes in a wide range of colours - purple, red, pink and white. Height: 9in, Spread: 9in.

Armeria maritima

This is well known as thrift and forms tufts of grass-like foliage which form into round mounds. The flowers are pink, red or white and appear in early summer. This neat and tidy growing plant grows about 5in high with a 6in spread.

Lewisia cotyledon

Forming an evergreen rosette, the flowers are in shades of pink, orange, purple, apricot and white, and appear in early summer. This makes an ideal crevice plant. Available in different sizes but can grow up to 1ft high with a 9in spread.

Lithodora diffusa 'Heavenly Blue'
This makes an evergreen spreading small shrub, which produces a profusion of rich sky blue flowers in summer. It can grow 6 to 8in high and can spread from 1 to 2ft.

Aubrietia
One of the most popular of all rock garden plants, known for its brilliant display from March to early June. After flowering, make sure to trim to ensure neat, bushy plants. Named varieties offer a good choice of different colours which are usually purple, lilac, mauve, white and red. Height: 4in, Spread: 12in.

Campanula carpatica
Flowers from June through to August, making a low bush plant with attractive cup or saucer-shaped flowers which are available in various shades of blue and also white. Height: 5in, Spread: 10in.

Erysimum cheiri 'Harpur Crewe'
Old-fashioned double yellow wallflower. Sweetly scented. Height: 2ft, Spread: 1ft.

Erysimum cheiri 'Harpur Crewe'

Helianthemum
Commonly called rock rose. Small, shrubby plant best in a sunny position. There are many named varieties available ranging in colour from red, pink and white through to yellow and orange and varying shades in between. There are also some double-flowered forms. The foliage ranges from green to silver. Height: 1ft, Spread: 1ft.

Ophiopogon planiscarpus nigrescens
An outstanding black grass-like plant. Slow-spreading, making a low mound and producing short spikes of tiny pale-pink flowers. Height: 6in, Spread: 1ft.

Primula denticulata
Commonly known as the drumstick primula. Enjoys a moist position. Comes in white, pink and red. Height: 1ft, Spread: 6in.

Rhodohypoxis baurii
This South African gem is an ideal trough plant, coming in red, white and pink. Best dried off in winter when the bulbs are dormant. Flowering from May to late summer, making good sized clumps when established. Best divided in April. Height: 3in, Spread: 8in.

Pink Rock Rose

Primula denticulata

Rhodohypoxis

Hints

Primula auricula 'Marigold'

Protection

Prop a sheet of glass over the buds of early-flowering rock garden plants to protect them from frost damage.

Sowing Seeds

Sow seed of gentians and other alpines in late autumn and leave the seed pots outdoors over winter when the frost and winter cold will break the seed's dormancy.

Construction 1

When constructing a rock garden use rocks of the type that occur locally. Other rocks can look out of place.

Greenhouse

When growing alpines in a greenhouse you will not need heating. Provide as much ventilation as possible. Think of your alpine greenhouse as a large, well-ventilated cloche.

Construction 2

The best time for building a rock garden is in autumn so that the stones can settle into the ground by spring.

Irrigation

During the growing season rock plants require plenty of moisture, particularly those on a south-facing slope. In order to ease this work an irrigation system can be built in during the construction of the rock garden.

Weeds

Remove weeds even in their youngest stage of growth from the rock garden throughout the year.

Sempervivum in trough

Care Calendar

May
Weed the rock garden thoroughly with a handfork or small trowel. Add a fertiliser to rosette-forming rock plants and apply a top dressing to the entire rock garden to improve the soil.

June
Water in the evening during dry spells. Take cuttings of plants in pots that have finished flowering.

July
Collect and store seed for sowing now or later in the year.

August
Take cuttings and keep them shaded during hot weather.

January
Sow seeds that need frost for germination.

February
Add a top dressing of gravel or grit around plants in the rock garden. This ensures free drainage. Check for slugs, especially around early-flowering bulbs.

March
Plant rock plants as soon as possible. Check plants in pots for vine weevil.

April
Prick out winter sown seedlings into pots. Divide early-flowering plants kept in a cold greenhouse.

September
Transplant any plants that need to be moved, making sure to water well before and after. Plant dwarf bulbs for spring flowering.

October
Prepare for winter by covering tender plants.

November
Clean fallen leaves from the rock garden.

December
Sow seeds in pots with good drainage and leave outside to overwinter.

Saxifraga 'Southside Seedling'

Chives in flower

Herbs

There is something special about growing and using your own herbs, whether for medicinal or culinary use. Herbs can make a valuable contribution also to the ornamental garden as many are attractive plants which not only add colour but also scent. The main requirement for the majority of herbs grown is a sunny spot in well-drained, fertile soil. Even if you have limited space there is still an opportunity to grow herbs, as many of the popular types can easily be grown in tubs or containers.

Planting

Before planting herbs it is essential to prepare the soil in advance. This work should be carried out in early autumn. Cover the ground with well-rotted manure or homemade garden compost, creating a 3in layer. Once covered, dig this in. In the following spring lightly fork the bed over a couple of weeks before planting. There is no need to add artificial fertiliser. Many herbs, especially those from the warmer Mediterranean areas, grow better and with stronger flavour if they are left slightly short of nutrients.

A Herb Wheel

An attractive way of growing a selection of low-growing herbs is to use an old method which is often used by cottage gardeners— laying a cart wheel on the ground which divides a circle into segments for the different herbs you wish to grow. This can look especially effective if raised up on a circle of red bricks, adding a little extra height.

Prepare the ground by digging and manuring before the wheel is put in place. Make sure that the site is free-draining and in sun. Create a solid weed-free area around the wheel in the form of a path which could be made from gravel. This will give you easy access when harvesting the herbs.

Plant the individual segments with different

varieties. Make sure to avoid plants that would become too big as they will soon overtake their smaller neighbours. By cleverly selecting herbs with different coloured foliage you can make a very attractive and functional display.

Preserving Herbs

During summer, it is important to preserve some of your herbs for winter use. Herbs can be picked and tied in bunches to dry in a warm room. They can look decorative while drying and have the advantage of being close to hand when needed.

Freezing herbs retains more of their fresh flavour. Place a small amount in clear plastic bags, either whole or chopped. They should be ready for use. These can be frozen and used as required.

If you are conscious of flavour, you can retain more of this if you freeze your herbs in ice cubes. The cubes with the herbs can be added directly to sauces and casseroles. You also have the option of using mint leaves frozen in ice cubes at any time of year, especially in summer when they can be used to cool drinks.

Herbs on the Windowsill

Herbs can easily be grown on the kitchen windowsill provided that you do not mind replacing them on a regular basis as they will not be a long-term proposition in small pots. The ease of access makes it very attractive to have three or four pots to hand. The best for a windowsill are chives, basil, thyme, parsley and mint.

Mint

Six Favourite Herbs

Chives *(Allium schoenoprasum)*

Good as a low edging plant for borders, this attractive herb can also be used in winter when forced. The mild onion flavour makes it ideal for garnishing and for flavouring salads. Complements soft cheeses, beautiful in soups and also ideal for dips. The flowers make a very attractive addition to salads.

When to Harvest Your Herbs

Herb	Which part to use	When to use it fresh	When to cut for preserving
Basil	Leaves	July - September	Just before flowering
Bay	Leaves	All year round	All year round
Borage	Young leaves and flowers	All summer	Whenever there are suitable young shoots
Chervil	Leaves	Summer	Summer, before flowering
Chives	Leaves	May - September	When leaves have reached full size
Dill	Leaves and seeds	All summer from successional sowings	Just before flowering for foliage. Gather seedheads just before they ripen
Fennel	Leaves and seeds	All summer	July - October
Lemon Balm	Leaves	June - September	June - September
Marjoram	Leaves and flowers	July - September	July - September
Mint	Leaves	June - October	Just before flowering
Parsley	Leaves	All summer	June - July
Rosemary	Leaves	All year round	June - August
Sage	Leaves	June - October	Just before flowering
Sorrel	Leaves and shoots	May - August	Before flowering
Tarragon	Leaves	June - September	June - September
Thyme	Leaves and flowers	June - September	Before and at flowering time

Fennel

Chives

French Tarragon (*Artemesia dracunculus*)

This is a half-hardy shrubby plant which needs a sheltered sunny spot in alkaline soil if it is to do well. The foliage is often used in *sauce béarnaise* and is a wonderful complement to chicken dishes and eggs, often used to flavour vinegar.

Borage (*Borago officinalis*)

An attractive upright annual needing sun and well-drained soil. The cucumber-flavoured leaves and flowers can be added to cold drinks. Wonderful when used with Pimms. The flowers are often used crystallised as cake decoration.

Coriander (*Coriandrum sativum*)

Attractive, finely-divided foliage suitable for growing in sun or semi-shade. Used in popular Thai cooking, the spicy flavour is also used in curries and is excellent when used in chutneys too.

Bay (*Laurus nobilis*)

The evergreen bay makes an ideal topiary, making a very attractive year-round focal point in a herb garden. The leaves are most commonly used in *bouquet garni*. Bay leaves are also used with meat and fish dishes and have a popular addition when flavouring stocks and marinades.

Basil (*Ocimum basilicum*)

This half-hardy annual, which requires warmth to germinate and grow well, is excellent as a windowsill pot plant. The leaves are used in tomato and pasta dishes. It is essential for pesto and is often used in salads and vinegars.

Standard Wisteria with herbs

Hints

Preserving Herbs

If you do not have space to grow parsley and other herbs in winter a simple method of preserving them is by freezing. This can be done in an ice cube tray.

Mint

For the best mint sauce use woolly-leaved apple mint. For new potatoes, spearmint is better.

Borage

Use the rich blue flowers of borage to add interest to cold drinks. Drop single fresh flowers into the water in each of the compartments in an ice cube tray.

Tarragon

This is delicious with chicken. Make sure when buying that you select French tarragon and not Russian.

Buying Herbs

Almost all types of herbs are best bought as named varieties which have been raised from cuttings rather than from seed.

Garlic

Pot up a few garlic cloves in spring and keep them on the windowsill or in a greenhouse. They will supply you with green shoots for flavouring.

Thyme

For the best thyme to combine rich flavour and also an attractive appearance look for the bushy variety 'Silver Posy'.

Care Calendar

January

Prepare the ground for planting new herbs when weather allows.

February

Sow parsley in pots under glass. Propagate mint by runners.

March

Sow basil in a heated propagator. Divide and replant large clumps of perennial herbs. Prune back shrubby herbs to produce new shoots and leaves.

April

Continue to sow seed, including basil, under glass. Position stakes to support large plants such as lovage and comfrey. This is a good time to start planting a new herb garden.

May

Take softwood cuttings of shrubby herbs. Start harvesting chives and other salad herbs. Pot on basil plants into large pots of good quality compost to encourage quick growth.

June

Continue sowing salad herbs. Also, biennial and perennial herbs. Position tender herbs in containers in warm sheltered corners of the garden.

July

Lift garlic bulbs, bunch loosely and hang in an airy place to dry. Cut lavender to dry.

August

Harvest herb seed. Continue harvesting culinary herbs for freezing or drying for winter use.

September

Sow parsley and chervil for winter use. Lift clumps of chives, French tarragon, mint and sorrel and plant in pots to be brought inside later for winter use. Trim lavender and sage to tidy up for winter. Plant garlic cloves in deeply-cultivated garden soil.

October

Tidy herb garden. Leave a little old growth for winter protection. Finish planting garlic cloves. Plant hardy herbs if soil is still warm.

November

Clear fallen leaves from plants. Check crops under glass for pests.

December

Bring herbs for winter use indoors if not yet done.

Desert Cacti

Cacti & Other Succulents

I have always had a great love of cacti and succulent plants, and as a young boy I amassed a large collection over many years which gave me great pleasure and also taught me a lot about cultivating these plants. Some of the first plants I ever grew from seed on a windowsill at the age of eight were several cacti. These amazed me as they were easy to grow and were quite tolerant of neglectful periods when I forgot to water them. They really are incredibly forgiving plants, providing you do not put them through harsh extremes.

Echinocactus (Golden Barrel Cactus)

Cacti are those plants with spines and these come from the 'New World', Mexico being a very big source. Succulents are those without spines and come from the 'Old World', with great numbers coming from South Africa. Many of them have spectacular flowers and, if treated with care and given the correct growing conditions, the rewards can be as spectacular as the most flamboyant orchids.

I remember being told when very young that it took a cactus seven years to bloom and it would not flower again for another seven years. This is one of those myths that I am happy to tell you is not true, for cacti and succulent plants, if selected especially for their flowers, will reward you with an annual display. Sometimes only for a brief period, but the show is always good.

My mother grew another cactus which is very popular in this country – the Christmas Cactus. This differs from other types in that it is known as an epiphyte and generally grows on the side of trees, where it collects moisture from rain. It is from this plant, which she had for many years, that I learned how to take cuttings. Some of the earliest cuttings I took, apart from geraniums, were of the Christmas Cactus.

Cacti and succulents, when grouped together, make very attractive collections. One plant on its own can be brought to life with the addition of others. Both cacti and succulents work well together as they like similar growing conditions. For enthusiasts, there are specialist nurseries who mail order plants and in Ireland there is a special society devoted to the growing of these fascinating plants. A great joy of creating a collection is the sharing and swapping of information and also the exchanging of plants. To discover how one person grows a plant to perfection where you may not have done so well is always a learning experience.

Cacti and succulents are not difficult to grow and if you follow a few simple rules you will have years and years of pleasure from these remarkable plants.

Desert Cacti

These plants come from arid regions of South America and North America. The name desert suggests that they come from deserts, but this is generally not true. Desert cacti, as they are collectively known, are those with spines and watering should be reduced, if not stopped completely, from the middle to the end of October until the end of March or early April. Expose these plants to full sunshine. It is essential if they are to flower. They make ideal plants for a conservatory, greenhouse or a south-facing windowsill.

Forest Cacti

Forest Cacti

This group of plants, which include the Christmas Cactus, naturally grow in the tropical forest regions of America. They are known as epiphytes and can be found growing naturally on trees. They are not parasites but use the trees for support. They are easy to recognise by their trailing growth and their usually flattened, leaf-like stems. At the hottest times of year this group of plants require a little shade and are ideal for placing in east or north facing windowsills. They can be placed outside during summer in shady spots. To encourage them to flower it will be necessary to water and apply a light liquid feed during the winter months.

Succulents

These plants, which include hundreds of different types, are generally not spiny. They have succulent leaves which store water. The majority come from Africa, with South Africa being a particularly rich source. As with desert cacti, it is rare to find them growing in desert regions, but they are accustomed in their natural habitat to fairly arid conditions. They

Echinocactus grusonii

Care – The Basics

Temperature

The majority of plants will require frost-free conditions. It will be necessary to bring plants that are grown on a windowsill into the room during the coldest parts of winter. Cool and frost-free is ideal.

Watering

It is necessary during their growing period, from April to September, to provide adequate water for their growth. This will mean watering but allowing the plant to dry between watering, but not leaving the plant dry for any great length of time. The trick is regular watering while the plant is in growth, but allowing it to dry fully between each watering.

also require little or no water between October and the following March. Watering is only given to prevent the plant completely dehydrating. The majority appreciate full sunshine and are happy when placed on a south-facing windowsill or in as much light as possible.

The vast majority of these plants, especially those from warmer countries, are not frost tolerant. They will cope with cold conditions in winter only if kept on the dry side. It is necessary with all to provide cool but frost-free conditions with as much light as possible through winter.

Echinopsis Sp.

Mammillaria

Repotting

Young plants may require an annual repotting. Older plants can often survive being pot-bound but will require an occasional liquid feeding. When repotting it is important to use a free-draining compost. It may be necessary to add extra grit or sharp sand to give adequate drainage.

Desert Cacti

Astrophytum

A choice and attractive plant, often with few spines. Attractive flowers are produced throughout the summer, often rich yellow with a red centre. Careful cultivation is required to get the best from this plant.

Echinocactus

Commonly referred to as the Barrel cactus, these over a long time can make large plants weighing over 1000kg. Flowers vary from yellow to pink. Growth is extremely slow, but these plants are very easy to grow. They can be prone to rot so careful watering is essential.

Opuntia

Echinopsis

Plants can vary from small and dwarf to big giants, and the flowering colours range across all that can be found in the Cactaceae. There are beautiful hybrids available that make ideal windowsill plants.

Mammillaria

This is one of the largest genera with over 250 species, making it one of the most popular and widely available. Flowers can range in colour from cream through to pink and red.

Opuntia

This is often commonly called the Bunny's Ear cactus because of the shape it develops. Another common name is Prickly Pears. This name describes the spiny, edible fruit. There are many different types and the spines are quite ferocious. Flowers can be orange, red or yellow. The geographical range of this plant is from Canada to Argentina.

Rebutia

This is one of my favourites because of its free-flowering nature. They are generally small plants. The flowers are some of the most spectacular, especially when you see a plant in full flower. The colour range is wide – purple, red, orange, yellow and white.

Forest Cacti

Epiphyllum hybrid (Orchid Cactus)

This is one of the most spectacular flowering cacti you can grow. It bears large flowers in a very wide range of vivid colours. The genus is found mainly in Mexico and Central America. A plant in full flower is truly spectacular.

Zygocactus truncatus (Christmas Cactus)

One of the most popular indoor houseplants, commonly known as the Christmas Cactus. Easy to grow, requiring a little shade, and also needing a moderate watering and feeding during winter. It can be put outside in a sheltered, shady spot in the summer.

Rebutia

Agave

Succulent Plants

Agave
This is a large genus of rosette-forming succulents, many of which can grow extremely large, though dwarf species are available. They are usually monocarpic. This means that after flowering the plant dies. Flowering takes many, many years.

Aloe
Coming from Madagascar and Africa, the most usual growth form for this plant is a rosette of thick leaves. *Aloe vera* is a popular member of this group and its sap is often used in cosmetics and herbal medicine.

Crassula
This is also a large genus. One of the most popular is a common houseplant known as the Money Tree or Jade Tree.

Echeveria
Leafy succulents which come from Mexico and South America. Some have attractively coloured foliage. They are easily propagated, often by division of offsets.

Euphorbia
Euphorbia contains over 2000 species not all of which are succulents. Succulent varieties occur in Madagascar, the Canary Islands, and Africa. There are many and varied forms including the attractive *Euphorbia obesa* which is one of the most popular and interesting of the group. It is almost extinct in the wild but is well represented in collections.

Sansevieria
Commonly known as the Mother-in-Law's Tongue, this plant comes from Africa and India. It is a very popular houseplant and is usually purchased in its variegated form, which has yellow stripes and markings on the leaves. Propagation is usually by division of offsets, but leaf cuttings can also be taken.

Hints

Transplanting

When transplanting a thorny cactus, a folded piece of newspaper can come in handy. Fold this and then wrap it around the centre part of the thorny plant, leaving enough paper to grip. This means you can move the plant securely without risk of it toppling over and causing damage. This method makes it easy to manoeuvre the plant while potting, protecting both you and the plant from damage.

Agaves

Agaves have very sharp thorns on the end of each leaf. These can be potentially dangerous to children and pets. You can remove the tips with a sharp secateurs, but this is still not a sufficient protection. Another method is to use old wine bottle corks which can be secured to the top of each leaf by pressing them onto each spike.

Potting

When potting cacti and succulents, always provide extra drainage in the bottom of the pot. For large pots, pieces of polystyrene will give you the necessary drainage without adding weight to the container.

Feeding

During the growing season, many flowering cacti and succulents will benefit from an occasional

Christmas Cactus

application of liquid tomato feed. This can encourage flowering.

Miniature Garden

A miniature garden can be created using small cacti and succulents. Cover the bowl with fine gravel and select a nice stone or rock for the centre. This miniature garden can be fun for children to create.

Summer Holidays

Cacti and succulents can be moved outdoors in summer. Position them in the sunniest spot. A group on a table of different sizes can make an attractive display and when you're on holiday they will look after themselves.

Rebutia

Strawberries

Soft Fruit-
Strawberries & Raspberries

It is hard to think of anything more delicious than picking your own soft fruit, whether to be eaten fresh or to make jams or preserves. There is nothing quite the same when it comes to the flavour of homegrown fruit. By growing at home you have control over the varieties you grow. You can often choose some of the old-fashioned types which were developed for their excellent flavour. In some cases, the crop may not be quite as abundant, but this is made up for when it comes to taste.

It is well worthwhile going to a little extra trouble when preparing the soil as the work you put in will most definitely be repaid when it comes to harvest time. The taste of freshly picked strawberries or just the joy of spreading your own blackcurrant jam makes it all worthwhile.

Strawberries

When it comes to strawberries for me it is all about the variety. I detest the supermarket strawberries, which seem to be available all year round. For me, strawberries should be in season and taste of strawberries. I remember the first time I grew 'Royal Sovereign'. I was astonished by its spectacular flavour – truly outstanding. The fruits vary in size from small to large and are often slightly wedge-shaped. The yield is not very high and the life

Strawberries

of the plants is rather short as this old variety becomes rapidly virused, a disease which ends the life of the plants. But despite the problems associated with this old variety it still sets the benchmark when it comes to that delicious taste that is the essence of summer.

Growing

In general, strawberries are not too fussy about soil once it is fertile and well drained. For planting, select a position that is protected from wind. Avoid planting them in shade, especially the shade of trees and shrubs, and at all costs the north facing side of a wall is to be avoided. If you plant in a very sunny, warm spot remember that young plants and those coming into fruit may require extra watering during hot spells.

Strawberries should be 'rotated'. This means not always growing them in the one position. The ground should be let rest for as long as possible, certainly several years between planting. If the ground has been well prepared with organic matter before planting it will most definitely benefit the quality of plants, fruit and flavour. Avoid following potatoes when planting strawberries if you are rotating as disease can spread from one to the other. Strawberry plants will start to produce runners in June. This starts after flowering. Remove these using secateurs.

Make sure to keep the strawberry bed free of weeds as these will compete with the plants and cause you problems later.

Each year, your strawberry plants will produce two sets of leaves. The first set of leaves will appear in spring. The purpose of this is so that the plant can support the fruit. A second set is developed in late summer into autumn, and this set the plant uses to build up new strong crowns for the following year's crop. So after the plants have finished fruiting all the leaves should be cut off as close to the crown as possible. In late winter, the autumn set of leaves can be cut off, though if you are growing perpetual fruiting strawberry varieties avoid cutting off any leaves after July. In this case, only remove decayed leaves or those showing signs of disease.

Planting Runners

When buying strawberries, they are often purchased as established runners or sometimes one-year-old plants. Planting is best carried out with a trowel or if you wish you can use a small border spade. This can be used to open a 'V' slit about 6in deep in the soil. Place the base of the crown of the runner on the edge of the slit with the roots pointing down to their longest or fullest extent. Avoid having the roots curling upwards. They need to be pointing downwards. If you find that the roots on the runners are a little too long they can be cut back, but no shorter than 4 to 5in. Always use a sharp secateurs for this job. The soil then can be pulled back onto the roots and firmed in using the heel of your boot.

Strawberries in pots

It is important that runners are planted at the correct depth. Avoid having the crown sitting too high above the soil. Likewise, avoid planting the crown too deeply. In the first year of planting it may be necessary to remove the flowers, especially if growth is poor or slow. If growth is healthy and strong it is possible to get a light crop. The flowers can be nipped off using a scissors. By doing this in the first year you provide energy for the strawberry plants to build up stronger crowns which are more likely to produce a bumper crop the following year.

Recommended Varieties

'Cambridge Late Pine'
This is regarded as one of the classic old British varieties. Very sweet, juicy, firm fruits, which are a beautiful dark, crimson colour. The flavour is excellent.

'Ellsanta'
A newer variety which is one of the better varieties used by commercial growers. Believed to supersede Cambridge Favourite. Large, attractive looking fruits with very good flavour.

'Florence'
Also a new variety, producing a late crop of excellent quality fruit. Outstanding disease resistance. Dark red fruits of good size and heavy cropping. Not fussy about soil. Very good flavour.

Raspberries

If you carefully select varieties of raspberry, you can have early, mid-summer and late season cropping. This means that you can stagger fruiting from the end of June well into October. Some varieties are excellent for freezing. It will be important, as with all soft fruit, to protect the raspberries from birds, unless you have the space to grow enough for wildlife and your pleasure too. Special netting can be bought and a frame can be made to keep the birds at bay.

Raspberries are really grown where space allows. In a small, modern, tiny garden they are not really suitable, but where you have the space they are best planted in rows in an open, sunny position. When they start cropping you can enjoy a bowl of fresh raspberries with a light sprinkling of sugar and cream. Keeping it simple is the key to enjoying these delicious fruits.

Rasberry

Planting

Raspberries most definitely benefit from well-prepared soil before planting the canes. Good drainage is paramount. It is a good idea when planting the rows to dig out a trench 18in wide by 2ft deep. Prepare the soil, allowing it to settle before planting. When planting the canes placing them at the correct depth is essential if you are to get good growth in the first year. The uppermost roots on the canes should be no more than 2in below soil level. The white growing buds may be as high as the soil level. After planting make sure that the roots are firmed in well. This will also help to prevent rocking of the canes. The canes, if not already cut, should be cut back to approximately 9 in. I find this is best done prior to planting if not immediately afterwards.

Support

When supporting the rows of raspberries, it is a good idea to use posts and wire. This can be simply put in position making sure that the posts are bedded in firmly. Posts need to be a little over 6ft in height. These should be driven into the ground to a depth of a little over 1ft. Twelve gauge wire should be used to support the canes.

To get the very best yield from your raspberries it is necessary to control the number of canes. Ten per metre of row is ideal. Thinning can be carried out in early May and again in June when the canes are approximately 18in tall. If too many canes are produced you may need to dig some of them up. Avoid cutting them off at ground level.

Pruning

Raspberries which are summer-fruiting varieties can be pruned after the crop has been harvested. Pruning can really be carried out any time up until the end of the following January. The ideal time is August or September when you can tie in the new canes, which are more readily pliable at this time. The pruning is simple: cut out with a secateurs each cane which has already been cropped leaving the smallest possible stub at the base.

For autumn-fruiting varieties, those that crop from late summer into October on the previous seasons canes, each winter all the canes that have fruited are cut down to ground level. So do not allow any of the canes that have produced an autumn crop to grow over winter.

Recommended Varieties

'Malling Jewel'

Considered by many as the best variety, certainly grown for more than thirty years. Tolerant of virus infection. A moderate cropper with good, compact habit. This raspberry is easy to manage. The conical shaped raspberries are dark red and firm. Fruits ripen over a period of between three and four weeks. The flavour is very good.

'Glen Magna'

This is a late to mid-season variety which gives a very heavy yield. Fruit is dark red with an exceptionally good flavour. This raspberry is superb for freezing. The growth is upright and strong. This variety has good disease resistance.

'Autumn Bliss'

My favourite autumn-fruiting variety. This is the last of the summer-ripening types with good-sized berries of a rich red colour. Firm with good flavour. Best grown in a sheltered spot.

Ornamental Grasses

Hakonechloa

Grasses are among the many plants that have captured everyone's imagination, especially in the design of contemporary gardens. They are airy, light and easy to grow. They provide grace and beauty and are unique among perennial plants. By simply incorporating ornamental grasses into a planting scheme the mood of the garden can be transformed. They are equally at home when used in formal or informal settings. As plants, they are undemanding and generally require very little maintenance.

Recommended Grasses

Hakonechloa macra 'Alboaurea'
One of the most graceful of golden variegated grasses, *Hakonechloa* forms a low mound of dense, hanging foliage. The leaves are golden yellow and are striped green. Tiny flowers are produced in early autumn. It can be found growing in the wild as a rare endemic of wet, rocky cliffs in the mountains of the capital Tokaido district of Honshu from Sagami to Kii province. Grow this plant in light shade as full sunshine can discolour the foliage. It prefers rich, fertile soil which does not dry out.

Milium effusum 'Aureum' (Bowle's Golden Grass)
This is a treasure of the early spring garden. It is a perennial which forms loose tufts and the soft, limp foliage is a brilliant golden yellow. For best effect, grow this grass in shade where the colour of the leaves retains its brilliance for much longer into the season. It is happy in fertile soil and enjoys moderate moisture. It will seed without becoming a nuisance.

Stipa gigantea

Festuca glauca

Forms tight cushion mounds of about 9in across. The foliage is soft and needle-like and in the best forms is almost an iridescent blue. Flowering stems appear in late spring until mid summer. Must have full sun in a well-drained soil. This plant will not tolerate wet winters if there is bad drainage.

Stipa gigantea

Regarded as among the most beautiful of ornamental grasses this makes an excellent specimen. It is sometimes called the Spanish Oat Grass and forms a clump making a dense, low mound of dark green foliage. In late spring large panicles rise from this clump on 6ft stems. The flower heads shimmer when caught by sunlight as they move in the breeze making it one of the most spectacular garden plants you can grow. Grow this plant in the sunniest spot you have. When established it is quite drought resistant, but it is recommended to water well while the plant is settling in.

Cortadiera selloana (Pampas Grass)

One of the most popular of ornamental grasses. In recent years, variegated versions have also appeared on the market. It forms large clumps which make attractive arching mounds. From these rise flamboyant plumes which look stunning when lit from behind by sunshine. Also can look great when positioned against a dark background, for example a yew hedge. For best results, plant in full sun with rich, well-drained soil.

Miscanthus

A highly fashionable grass. A large number of selected cultivars, many of which were raised on the continent, have become available over the last few years. Generally tall-growing. Several very handsome variegated forms are available, such as 'Cosmopolitan' and 'Cabaret'. Stunning when in full flower, producing airy plumes which, when planted in groups, create a beautiful effect when caught by a light breeze. They can be slow to establish, requiring well-drained, fertile soil in a sunny position.

Mixed Grasses

Copper Beech

Hedges

Hedges are a very important and often an integral part of gardens. Their uses range from the practical through to the ornamental. They create living barriers which provide shelter and privacy. They also can be effective noise barriers and when it comes to style you can choose from both formal and informal to complement your overall garden. The secret of success when it comes to selecting a hedge to suit your garden is to make sure that you have the necessary space and you put in a little effort in advance when it comes to preparing the soil for planting. After that it is simply annual maintenance which keeps your hedge looking well.

New Yew Hedge

Preparation & Planting

As hedges are a permanent division and feature of your garden it is important to prepare the soil thoroughly in advance of planting. Hedging plants, once established, will also benefit from a general fertiliser or mulch, which can be applied each spring. When planting young hedging, bare root plants are often available in the autumn. At this time and other times you may also have the choice of container grown hedging. This may cost a little more, but will establish quickly. Hedging should be planted in a single row in a trench of approximately 1 to 2ft in width. Larger plants may require up to 3ft in width, depending on the size of container or root ball. Double rows can also be used, but this is more unusual. They can be used in the case of creating a noise barrier or where animals are being separated from garden. Young hedging plants are very vulnerable to drying out in their first season so it is essential after planting that regular watering is provided until they have established. Mulching is beneficial in that it helps to retain moisture. It also cuts down on weeds which may compete with young plants. It is a good idea to prepare the trench for planting in advance. This allows it to settle. Dig well-rotted manure into the bottom of the trench and use a general slow-release fertiliser when back filling the trench. When planting, follow the planting distances recommended for each type.

Recommended Varieties

Evergreen

Buxus sempervirens (Box)

This is one of the most popular hedging plants for use in formal settings. It is excellent for outlining the shape of beds, edging pathways and it also can be clipped into shapes. The planting distance should be approximately 12in between plants and trimming should be two to three times a year during the growing season. Old box hedging, with care and feeding, will respond well to renovation. It can be clipped to a height of 1 to 2ft. Sometimes there are dwarf varieties available which can be kept as low as 6 to 12in high. It is evergreen and there are variegated forms available.

Escallonia

Escallonia is an excellent flowering hedge which can be formally trimmed or left informal. It is a good choice for coastal areas as it will tolerate sea breeze. Clipping is immediately after flowering in summer. Planting distance should be approximately 18in apart and it makes an ideal hedge to clip to a height of 4 to 8ft. Old hedges respond well to renovation.

Box Hedge

Ilex aquifolium (Holly)

Holly is a popular choice and though it can be relatively slow-growing it makes a dense and effective barrier which is appropriate where extra security is required. It is tough and resilient. Planting should be approximately 18in between plants and you can expect to trim a hedge to a height of 6 to 12ft. Clipping should be in late summer and it responds well to renovation.

Lavendula (Lavender)

Lavender is an excellent low-growing, informal hedge for a sunny location. Planting distance should be approximately 12in apart and depending on the selected variety you can expect it to reach a height of between 18 and 36in. Clipping can be done twice – a light clipping in spring and another after flowering. Lavender does not respond well to renovation. It is best not to consider lavender as a long-term hedge as it may become woody and tired after five years.

Ligustrum (Privet)
One of the most widely grown hedges, available in plain green or variegated forms. Plant it 12in apart. It can be cut to a height of 5 to 10ft. It may need clipping up to three times in the growing season. Responds well to renovation.

Taxus baccata (Yew)
A superb evergreen hedge which is best planted as young plants at approximately 24in apart. It is generally grown to a height of between 4 and 12ft but can be grown taller. It is best clipped in summer and again in autumn. The dark green foliage of this hedge makes an excellent background to borders. It responds extremely well to renovation.

Thuja plicata 'Fastigiata'
This makes an attractive upright hedge. It should be planted at approximately 24in apart and can be cut to a height of 5 to 10ft. Clipping will be necessary in spring and early autumn. It does not regenerate well.

Pyracantha
Pyracantha can make both a formal and informal hedge. It has attractive berries in autumn and winter. Depending on the variety colours are available in orange, red or yellow. White flowers in early summer. Planting should be approximately 24in apart and clipping can be to an approximate height of 6 to 10ft.

Yew Hedge

Mixed Beech Hedge

Fuchsia magellanica

Deciduous fuchsias grow extremely well, especially in sheltered areas, making beautiful mid-summer to autumn flowering hedges. Planting distance should be 12 to 18in apart. It can be clipped into a formal shape, but looks best if there is space to allow it to develop an informal shape where the flowering can be fully appreciated. Height can vary, depending on variety, from 2 to 5ft. Pruning is carried out to remove old stems after flowering. Fuchsias regenerate extremely well.

Deciduous

Fagus sylvatica (Beech)

There are many different cultivars available. The most usually seen are purple or green-foliaged forms, the purple version often being called Copper Beech. Planting distance, depending on the size of the plants, can be from 12 to 24in apart. Height can be between 4 to 20ft and clipping is required once a year in late summer. It responds very well to renovation.

Rosa rugosa 'Roseraie de l'Haÿ'

An excellent informal hedge, ideal for coastal areas. Fragrant crimson flowers followed by large round-shaped rose hips. Planting distance is 18in apart and expect a height of approximately 5ft. In spring remove thin, twiggy pieces and generally tidy the plants. This rose has extremely fragrant flowers and is attractive from summer through to winter, when the hips can be fully appreciated. Also, a good security hedge because of its thorns.

Hints

When to Cut

Unless the weather is very mild, do not cut hedges before April or after October.

Birds' Nests

When cutting hedges in spring, especially for the first time, check that there are no birds nesting that you may disturb.

Box

Try to avoid cutting box too hard back into old wood. Unlike yew, it can often be slow to regenerate. You are better to cut back as far as you can go without cutting into very old wood.

Hedge and Topiary

Level Hedges

When you are cutting along the top of a hedge, erect a taught piece of string tied to two stakes and level this with a spirit level. Unless you have a very good eye for straight lines, this is the best way to have a perfectly straight cut hedge.

Tough Hedging

For a tough hedge, use hawthorn. It is strong and reliable.

Instant Privacy

If you want instant privacy and/or protection you may need to erect a fence alongside your newly planted hedge. In time the hedge will grow to the height you want, but if possible make sure to plant the new hedge on the sunny side of the fence.

Topiary

Topiary has been used in gardens for hundreds of years. It is the art of forming and shaping plants into ornamental or abstract shapes. The Romans used it and Louis XIV used it in his gardens, but it was really the Italians who made it their own. Today topiary can be seen in formal gardens throughout Europe.

Shaping

In today's context, topiary can help to add structure, looking especially well in the winter months when other plants have died back or are without leaves. It associates well with low hedging plants and is used extensively in containers. One of the most popular are standard bay trees which are clipped into 'lollipop' shapes and used in traditional Versailles tubs. Box hedging is clipped into a range of formal shapes such as globes, pyramids and corkscrew to name but a few.

For more elaborate shapes such as birds and animals a little more skill is required in training and keeping their shape. Today, specialist nurseries offer metal frames which act as a guide when training particular shapes. For simpler shapes, for example cones, bamboo canes can be used. Three bamboo canes made into a wigwam can be used as a rough guide for the formation of the conical shape. This is very suited to use with box hedging.

Topiary in Containers

When growing topiary in containers, once they have established it is important to use a liquid feed at fortnightly intervals through the growing season. This keeps the plant in good condition. Topiary can be grown in sun or shade, but if grown in containers in a shady spot it may be necessary to rotate the container every few weeks to keep the plants even and balanced.

Care

In winter it is necessary to remove snow from topiary, especially those of more complex shape. If topiary has a flat surface snow can gather and its weight may cause damage. As with all plant care it is necessary to mulch established plants in spring and to keep well watered during warm spells. Two or three applications of a general fertiliser through the growing season may be necessary for well-established specimens. Keep a close eye on weeds and make sure that individual specimen topiary does not have to compete with weeds or other garden plants which may damage the shape by overcrowding or compete for nutrients which may result in slowed down growth.

Topiary can be used to create symmetry in the garden. It can help to balance a view. Two formal shapes can be positioned to highlight an entrance or one specimen can be used as a focal point. Use topiary as you may use pieces of furniture in a room. By positioning carefully you can add to the visual impact of an area, and remember its twelve month value provides visual stability through the changing seasons.

Plants for Topiary

Buxus sempervirens (Box)

The most widely grown topiary plant. Extremely adaptable and easy for you to shape yourself, or you can buy ready-shaped in a wide range of different forms. Box regenerates very well and it is often possible to restore an older plant to its original shape, though usually somewhat larger. Will grow in sun or shade. Generally not fussy about soil, but it is worthwhile preparing the ground well in advance of planting. It is ideal for growing in containers, but it is important for established plants to be fed.

Ilex aquifolium (Holly)

This makes excellent large topiary pieces, for example pyramid shapes and standards. Variegated versions can look really good if positioned in front

Taxus baccata (Yew)

This is the classic topiary plant. Long-lived and versatile, it makes excellent large specimens. Best planted in the ground, though young plants can be grown in pots or containers for several years. Will grow in sun or shade in well-prepared, fertile soil.

For times of clipping and shaping, refer to hedging chapter.

of a darker background. Is best grown in the ground and not really suitable for containers long term. For berries it will be necessary to have male and female varieties in the vicinity. Feeding is important.

Yew Topiary

Geraniums on a windowsill

Propagation

Taking your own cuttings or propagating plants not only gives great pleasure but it allows you to increase your stock without extra cost, providing you with fresh plants for your garden or even plants to swap with neighbours and friends. Propagation adds great pleasure to gardening and when you start it's difficult to stop. Before you know it you will have your own nursery of baby plants. It is easy and a reliable way of guaranteeing the continuation of many plants you already grow.

Cold Frame

What You Will Need

Flowerpots – make sure they are clean and sterile.

Propagating Compost – It is best that compost used is low in nutrients as this will help to stimulate new root growth, which will go in search of food. I use 75% plain peat moss with no nutrient and 25% sharp grit or horticultural sand mixed well.

Rooting Hormone – This can be purchased in powder form or in liquid form. It is very important not to contaminate the rooting hormone so always separate a little from the main container. After using this small amount any excess should be discarded.

Remember it is a garden chemical so avoid inhaling or allowing it to come in contact with your skin. Handle with care and it is a good idea to use gloves.

Clear Polythene Bag – This acts as a little mini-greenhouse, helping to prevent the new cuttings from completely dehydrating. The bag should always be a clear one as coloured bags may prevent photosynthesis. I often use freezer bags that have self-sealing tops or small wire ties to close them.

Cold Frame – If you have space, a cold frame is very useful for propagation. It acts like a mini-greenhouse where you can protect seeds and cuttings while they develop. It is a good investment and it most definitely will pay for itself. It is not essential, but it is very useful.

Cuttings

Stem Cuttings

One of the easiest methods of taking cuttings is very simple and straightforward, and one I often use for *Pelargoniums* (geraniums). They're known as stem cuttings. These are taken later in the year, usually from June onwards. Remove a piece of non-flowering growth about 4 to 5in long from the tip of a shoot. Remove the lower leaves and cut just below a leaf joint with a sharp secateurs. Dip the cutting then into a little rooting hormone. Position in a pot in suitable compost. Water and cover with a clear polythene bag. Put the pot in a sheltered spot and wait for rooting. You will usually see roots appearing from the bottom of the pot and signs of growth will start.

Coleus

Regal Pelargonium

Rooting in Water

Some plants can be rooted in water. Often these have soft, fleshy stems, for example Busy Lizzies or Coleus. Fill a jar with water and cover the top of the jar with tinfoil. Make a few holes in the tinfoil and insert cuttings taken in the same way as for stem cuttings, except do not use the rooting hormone. It will be necessary to change the water if it becomes discoloured. Position the jar in a bright spot out of direct sunlight. Once roots start to appear move fairly quickly into compost as, if left to long, roots may become very brittle and not transplant so well.

Internodal Cuttings

This method is ideal for taking cuttings of clematis. It differs from stem cuttings as you cut between leaf joints instead of just underneath, hence the term internodal. Remove a section of stem from the clematis, trim between the leaf joints and leave about 2in below a pair of leaves. Trim off the top of the cutting immediately above the leaves. Place in suitable compost and cover the pot with clear polythene. Place in a sheltered, shaded spot. This method may take many weeks for rooting. Once rooted, the plants should be moved into another pot or into their permanent position.

Leaf Cuttings

This is a popular method when populating African Violets *(Saintpaulia)*, but it can also be used for taking cuttings of Christmas Cactus and *Sansevieria* (Mother-in-Law's Tongue). If you are taking leaf

African Violet

cuttings the job is best done in spring or early summer. Cut 2in of leaf stalk off the original plant using a very sharp blade. Avoid scissors as this can bruise and cause problems. Make a slightly slanted cut in the leaf stem. Lightly dip in rooting powder and make sure to shake off any excess. Insert the leaf stalk in moist sand and peat up to the base of the leaf. Water and cover with a clear polythene bag. Place on a window ledge in a spot that is not too sunny – bright but out of direct sunlight. The soil should be kept evenly moist, as with all cuttings. Wait for new growth to appear from the base and pot on.

Division

Dividing Rhizomes

Plants such as Bearded Irish have large, swollen roots known as rhizomes. Bearded Iris should be divided every two to three years, discarding the old and often exhausted centre and renewing the plants with the fresher, more vigorous outer rhizomes. Lift the irises after flowering in summer and cut off the young rhizomes from the old plant. Cut the leaves in half. This helps to prevent them being rocked by wind. Replant in a sunny position with the top of the rhizome being just above soil level, facing the sun. Water well and plants will establish quickly to develop a new colony the following year.

Dividing Perennials

Division of herbaceous perennial plants is best carried out in the autumn while there is still some warmth in the soil. The job can also be done in the spring just as you see the plants beginning to grow. Lift a clump using a fork and a spade. I find it best to place the clump on a large piece of polythene. Some clumps divide easily when you use two forks back-to-back. Some clump-forming plants, when divided, may need the central, older part discarded. Concentrate on the newer, outer growth for replanting. Plants with very fleshy roots, for example hostas and agapanthus, are best divided in spring. You may need to use an old carving or bread knife to cut the clump apart, again taking the outer new shoots. If you are replanting divisions it is always a good idea to revitalise the soil in that area. Adding some organic compost or even a little fresh topsoil will make all the difference.

Fuschia

the side of a branch, insert the seeds and seal with some soil.

Self-sown Seedlings
You can often find when weeding that there are self-sown seedlings under herbaceous perennials. These can be potted up and grown on to be used elsewhere. Also, annuals such as poppies may self seed. Some of these can be left to flower where they grow.

Drainage
When taking cuttings use a layer of sand on the top of the compost. This will ensure good drainage at the surface, which is needed.

Hints

Fuchsias
Take tip cuttings of fuchsias early in the year. They will root quickly and give you plenty of small plants ideal for bedding and containers.

Succulents
If you are separating offsets from succulents use a sharp knife to sever the connecting stem from the mother plant. Position the offsets on top of the compost bedded in a little sand. It will take several weeks for them to develop new roots.

Mistletoe
To get mistletoe to grow on an old apple tree you will need to insert ripe seeds, preferably growing in another old apple tree. Make a small slit into

Poppy Ladybird

Trained Pear

Tree Fruit

Tree fruit are very attractive. They provide flowers in early summer, and later in the season you benefit from the fruit. If you have the space you can develop an orchard where you have different fruits available, staggering the cropping or harvesting by carefully selecting different varieties. If you have a small garden it is possible to buy many different fruits, for example apples, which are specially grown on dwarfing root systems that keep the tree compact. You can also buy what is known as a 'family tree'. This is one tree where several different apples are grafted onto one stem providing you with different varieties in limited space. Also, it is worth considering growing fan-trained fruit where space is limited. These are purchased as specially trained trees suitable for growing against a wall. Plums and pears are excellent grown this way.

Apples

Planting

When planting always make sure to have the soil prepared well in advance as a fruit tree is fairly permanent. You can expect many years of pleasure and reward so it is worthwhile making every effort to have the soil in good condition before planting. The use of well rotted manure and decomposed garden compost will improve the texture of the soil and can be incorporated at planting time.

Select a well-drained, sunny spot and when planting make sure to plant to the same level that the tree had previously been at.

Feeding

All fruit benefits from an annual feeding as well as a mulch of well-rotted manure. You can also use a dressing of rose fertiliser as this is high in potash. The best time is in late winter or early spring.

Weeds

It is important to keep weeds and grass from the base, especially of newly-planted trees. A small piece of membrane can be cut and positioned around the tree to a radius of approximately 1ft. This porous membrane can be covered with a mulch.

Watering

It is crucial that your newly-planted trees receive enough water while they are establishing. Do not depend on rain. Also, established trees may need to

Plums

Plums are generally easy to grow. They can be grown as free-standing trees or trained against a wall. Plums are best eaten straight from the tree when you can really appreciate their delicious flavour. In a good year when the crop is heavy it may be necessary to thin some of the fruits. Also you may have to give extra support to branches on free-standing trees to help prevent damage from the extra weight of the crop.

Recommended Varieties

'Victoria'

This is the most popular variety and definitely the best one to have if you have only space for one plum tree. It is a heavy cropper with pale red fruits which are juicy and sweet. It is self-fertile. Pick August to September.

'Czar'

This is one of the best cooking plums. It has a rich, acidic flavour. The fruits are medium-sized and dark purple. It is self-fertile and should be picked in August.

'Opal'

Attractive red-purple fruits with a very juicy flesh and good flavour. It is a self-fertile variety and should be picked between July and August.

'Early Laxton'

One of the earliest to ripen. Excellent for use in dessert and cooking. Has a good flavour. Can be pollinated with 'Czar' or 'Victoria'. Pick in July.

'Denniston's Superb'

Large, rounded, golden fruits with a very good flavour. This variety performs well in colder gardens. It is self-fertile and fruit should be picked in August.

Hints

Crab apples

The addition of crab apples (Malus) can assist with pollination. They also have the benefit of the crab apple which can be used in autumn, and in spring their blossom makes an attractive feature.

Harvesting Apples

When harvesting apples, especially those for storage, make sure not to pull out the stalk. Get rid of any fruits which are showing signs of damage. Take a careful look to make sure there are no holes made by codling moth.

Propping up Branches

To prevent branches from breaking under the weight of fruit, put up a permanent wooden prop beneath the spreading branch. This will take the strain and prevent damage.

Pruning

Always walk around the trees when you are pruning. Make sure you are not cutting too much from one side. Try to keep a good overall shape.

Ripeness

Check apples for ripeness by gently lifting the fruit in the palm of your hand and lightly twist. When ripe the stalk will detach from the branch.

June Drop

Immature fruits will drop from your apple tree in early summer. This is called 'June Drop'. It is the tree getting rid of excess fruit which will never mature.

Storage

Always store apples away from pears, as pears need regular checking for ripeness. Apples are best left undisturbed.

Growing Against a Wall

Plant pear and plum trees against a wall. This provides protection and also encourages a good crop.

Bad Apples

Keep a close eye on apples as they ripen. All it takes is one bad apple to destroy the barrel.

Conservatory Plants

Conservatory plants differ from houseplants in that they need to tolerate greater temperature fluctuation, as a conservatory can be warm in the day and cool at night. They also need to be adaptable to growing in containers. Many have scented flowers which adds to the appreciation of their beauty at close quarters. The majority also have a long flowering period, giving interest and colour which is often valued in winter or early in the season. You will need to provide support for climbing types. Some of these can look well when suspended from wires across the roof of the conservatory. This often helps you to appreciate hanging flowers to full effect. Conservatory plants are generally easy to grow and providing they are fed using a liquid feed on a regular basis you will have many years of enjoyment and pleasure and will be able to transform your conservatory into an indoor paradise. These are some of my favourite recommended conservatory plants which have been tried and tested over time.

Abutilon

There are many different varieties, some of which will grow outdoors in a very sheltered spot, such as *Abutilon vitifolium*, but for the conservatory there are many tender varieties which provide a good show of flower throughout the summer. *Abutilon striatum*

Bougainvillea

'Thompsonii' has large foliage which is splashed with gold and green making a mosaic. The brightly coloured variegated foliage is complemented by orange bells.

Bougainvillea

Very showy and available in many rich colours. A typical sight growing outside in Mediterranean gardens. For bougainvillea to do well in a conservatory it must have a sunny position. Flowering can last a long time and they come in a wide range of pinks, reds, oranges, yellows and even white. Flowering can last well into the autumn. Regular feeding is required through the growing season.

Camellia

Excellent for a shady conservatory and requiring lime-free conditions. Double and single flowered forms are available in colours of red, pink and white. In time, camellias can make large conservatory plants which need appropriately sized pots. Feed through the growing season and give an annual iron tonic to help keep the foliage healthy and rich green.

Citrus

Oranges and lemons are the most popular citrus. They produce sweetly-scented white flowers which are followed by fruits which are edible. Lime-free soil is required and they should be allowed to slightly dry between watering. The most popular lemon is 'Meyer's Lemon' which tolerates cooler conditions than other varieties. It's important to provide good air circulation and to keep a close eye for red spider mite attack. A regular liquid feeding is important. Tomato feed can be used as this will encourage fruiting.

Clivia

An ideal plant for a shady conservatory. Arching, dark green, strap-shaped leaves form into a clump. The flowers are a rich orange and are usually carried above the foliage in spring. Clivia does not mind being pot-bound provided that you liquid feed. Avoid strong sunlight as this can bleach the foliage. If necessary, in summer move to a shady spot.

Clivia

Datura (Brugmansia)

A large, shrubby plant sometimes called the Angel's Trumpet as the flowers are trumpet shaped and hang beneath the leaves. There are several varieties ranging from white, pale pink and orange through to yellow. This is an easy and fast-growing plant which will also benefit from liquid feeding if grown in a container. Best propagated from cuttings. The plant is poisonous.

Gardenia

Beautifully scented white double flowers which turn to the most wonderful colour of Jersey cream. Rich, dark, glossy green leaves set off these flowers. This is a plant which requires year-round warmth and a

Orange

Lemon

Hoya carnosa

Evergreen climbing plant with succulent shiny foliage. White flowers hang in clusters. An easy to grow plant for sun or shade, but needs to be trained on a trellis or on wire. Well drained compost and regular liquid feeding is essential to encourage flowers.

Jasminum polyanthum

This climbing evergreen produces an abundant mass of pink buds which open to starry white

humid atmosphere. It dislikes sudden drops in temperature. Best grown in lime-free compost in light shade out of direct sunlight. Well worth taking every effort to grow for its exquisite scent.

Gloriosa

Commonly called the 'Flame Lily' this has to rank as one of the most exotic climbing plants you can grow. It needs support on which it will climb using tendrils from the tips of its leaves. It can grow to a height of 7 to 8ft high. Grown from a tuber planted in spring, provide good drainage and rich compost.

Gloriosa

Mandevilla 'Alice du Pont'

Plumbago

flowers, which have a fantastic scent, nearly overpowering at close quarters. In the conservatory this flowers in late winter. Needs support and regular watering and feeding to keep the plant in good condition.

Mandevilla (Dipladenia)

A stunning South American climbing plant which produces gorgeous funnel-shaped flowers. Look out for *Mandevilla* x *amabilis* 'Alice du Pont'. The flowers on this variety are a deep pink in bud opening to a lovely soft pale pink. Also needs support from trellis or wire. Can make a large climber. Happy in sun or light shade.

Passiflora antioquiensis (Passion Flower)

This passion flower stands out from the rest. A large growing plant with rich carmine pink to red coloured flowers which hang like parachutes from below the foliage. Needs plenty of room to grow and strong support. Best grown in a conservatory border rather than pot, but can be grown in a large container if space is limited. Requires annual pruning to prevent it from becoming too dense and overcrowded. Liquid tomato feed through the growing season will encourage flowers. In full flower this passion flower is spectacular.

Plumbago auriculata

A great favourite for its wonderful pale powder blue flowers. Like Bougainvillea it is often seen growing outside in Mediterranean gardens against walls. It flowers non-stop for weeks. Best grown against a wall in a conservatory. It is a fast-growing plant and may require a large pot as it matures. Can easily be grown from cuttings and in full flower a graceful and beautiful conservatory plant.

Strelitsia reginae (Bird of Paradise)
Exotic, flamboyant and spectacular describe the strangely beautiful flowers which resemble the head of a bird. The foliage is a rich green colour making a large clump. Excellent in a big pot, but needs full sun. Occasional feeding will encourage flowering. Tolerant of cool conditions in winter if kept on the dry side.

Tibouchina semidecandra
A large shrubby plant with evergreen foliage from Brazil. The flowers are an intense royal purple and are produced continuously on the plant, being especially valued in late winter. If allowed, without pruning it can reach a height of approximately 10ft. It may require pruning in smaller conservatories. Can also be grown against a wall, but will need support and tying in.

Strelitsia

Tibouchina

Scented Plants

Carnations

One area of gardening which is often neglected is that of scent. Gardening is very much a hands-on and visual subject so it is easy to neglect something that is not exactly tangible or that we can see. But through the course of my gardening work scent is one area which always captures people's attention when it comes to individual plants.

But how many of us actually plan or create a scented garden? Very few is the answer. So it is nice to take some time to think about the scent your garden provides and how you can take full advantage of the wonderful fragrance and aromas which plants can bring to the enjoyment of gardening. Every season has its own special scented plants. A scented flower or the aroma from a crushed leaf has the magical power of being able to transport you back in time, reminding you of a favourite place, happy moments, a person, a loved one, or just simply another era. So scent is important.

Today gardens are smaller and we must treat them in design as we would treat a room. In a way, our gardens have become an extension of our homes and the living space we use. Scented plants can enhance and add to the enjoyment of our garden use. A patio, terrace, decked area, a place where you sit or maybe even dine can be transformed with just a few easy-to-grow, fragrant plants. Here are some of my favourite scented plants, which can be grown individually or collected to provide fragrance throughout the year.

Daphne bholua
This rates very highly among my list of must-have plants. Its value comes into its own in winter when little else is in flower. Its fragrance is rich and sweet and loved by everyone who comes into contact with the plant. It makes an upright evergreen to semi-evergreen shrub. The leaves are rich, dark green. The flowers are small and can vary from white to rich pink. It is best positioned in a sheltered spot and, if possible, not too far from an entrance where the scent can be valued as one passes by while it is in full flower.

Sarcococca humilis (Christmas Box)
This rather inconspicuous plant has one of the most powerful fragrances for the winter garden. It is ideally suited to either sun or shade. It is evergreen

and the plants are low and compact. The flowers are rather insignificant, very tiny and usually cream or white. But what this plant lacks in appearance it more than makes up for with its fabulous and powerful fragrance, which drifts through the garden for yards, especially on a cold winter day. The fragrance is like créme brulee – burnt sugar and vanilla. Delicious and oozing as it spreads its sweet curds on the winter air.

Matthiola bicornis (Night-scented Stock)

If I was sent to a desert island and was allowed bring a few seeds the chances are they would be seeds of night-scented stock. In full flower it is not a showy plant, but the rich scent of cloves emitted by these tiny flowers at nightfall is so powerful that the fragrance can be detected for many yards from this small plant. There is no need to stoop to inhale their perfume for it will fill the air on a summer's evening, when the air is heavy and the night is calm. Sow the seed where it is to bloom, directly on prepared ground in March or April. It can be sprinkled in gaps between border plants, but make sure it is not too far from a path or a bench where you can appreciate it as you rest or pass.

Rosa 'Abraham Derby'

To describe the scent of a rose is a difficult task as there are so many different types of scented roses, so to pick out one that stands out from the crowd I can recommend R. 'Abraham Derby'. This is an English rose bred by David Austin. Its flowers are deeply cupped in shades of apricot, yellow and pink. They are large and are continuously produced through the summer. It is a strong-growing shrub rose and makes a bushy plant. The fragrance is very fruity with a refreshing sharpness. It is like uncovering a bowl of fruit salad with a hint of liquor.

Jasminum polyanthum

For a very sheltered wall or for a conservatory or glass porch, the number one climber for rich fragrance is *Jasminum polyanthum*. This early-

Hyacinth

flowering jasmine, when a large plant, produces thousands of pale pink buds which open to pure white stars. In a confined space the scent is so strong it can be found overpowering by some. Extraordinarily sweet and heavy, it is so strong that to be fully appreciated it needs to be diluted by the surrounding air as close inspection may take your breath away. For centuries, jasmine, like the scent of roses, has been used in perfumes and oils and has been valued as an expensive commodity. It is not a difficult plant to grow, but must have shelter from severe cold and bad weather if you are to appreciate the best it can offer.

Pelargoniums

There is an amazing range of scented-leaf pelargoniums (geraniums). In actual fact, if you find a specialist nursery catalogue you will quickly discover there are varieties with foliage scented of orange, chocolate, mint, rose, campher, lemon, and pineapple. These are old-fashioned plants and the pleasure of growing them is in appreciating the rich aromas which are released after you rub the leaves. They were often used to deter flies and were grown in pots on bathroom or kitchen windowsills to do this job. They all have flowers though primarily they are grown for the scent their foliage gives. To get the best from these they should be positioned in bright light, given well-drained compost and an occasional liquid feed during the growing season. The majority are easily propagated by taking cuttings and can be used during the summer months as part of bedding

Scented leaf pelargonium

plant schemes. They are wonderful when grown in tubs or containers and wonderful when positioned at the top of steps where you can run your hand through them as you pass by.

These are just the tip of the iceberg when it comes to the selection of really good scented plants. So the next time you visit a public garden, or even your garden centre, take some time to stop and appreciate the invisible world of scented flowers.

Scented Plants - A Quick Guide

Name	Scent
Anthemis nobilis (**Chamomile**)	Dull, sweet and fruity aroma, resembling a mixture of apples and bananas
Azara macrophylla	Strong vanilla scent
Clematis rehderiania	Delicate with a hint of cowslip
Cytisus battandieri	Pineapple aroma
Dianthus caryophyllus (**Carnation**)	Clove-like and sweet
Galanthus allenii (**Snowdrop**)	Almond scented
Galanthus nivalis	Mossy bouquet
Hyacinthus orientalis	Sweet and penetrating
Hesperis matronalis (**Sweet Rocket**)	Sweet and penetrating
Lathyrus odoratus	Richly sweet
Lavendula	Sweet and spicy
Lilium auratum	Sweet and strong
Lonicera x americana	Sweet and honey-like
Oenothera caspitosa (**Evening Primrose**)	Sweet and magnolia scented
Phlox paniculata	Very sweet
Rosa 'Penelope'	Musky-scented
Rosa 'Zéphirine Drouhin'	Raspberry-like
Rosa 'Constant Spry'	Strongly myrrh-like
Rosa 'Veilchenblau'	Rich orange scent
Wisteria floribunda	Vanilla-like and sweet

Sweet Pea

Weeds & Weed Control

Dandelion

I am often asked the question 'What is a weed?' The answer is simple. A weed really is just a plant growing in the wrong place, but of course there are many common weeds which are well known for the problems they cause by creating competition for other plants. If all of our garden plants were to grow like weeds there would be no problems in cultivating, especially more difficult-to-grow subjects.

If a garden is large enough, there is no harm in keeping an area for wilder plants and flowers which will attract wildlife. Many provide valuable food sources for insects such as butterflies. But in smaller gardens many of the common weeds are not desirable and if let run freely many can become a troublesome and recurring nuisance which adds to your gardening labours and chores. It is virtually impossible to eradicate weeds entirely, but with good management you can control weeds, bringing them to a level where they no longer become a troublesome nuisance.

Hand Weeding

Where a weed problem is not too bad hand weeding can be a very effective method of eradication. Make sure when removing weeds, especially perennial weeds, that you find all of the roots and eradicate them. In spring, a hoe is a very useful method for catching weed seedlings. Into early summer, the hoe is very effective. Use on a dry day when small weeds and weed seedlings will die through dehydration after being hoed. A hand trowel and hand fork are also very effective for dealing with weeds growing between valuable plants. Once the ground is clear of weeds in flowerbeds, using a mulch is an efficient way to prevent seedlings germinating as well as being beneficial to the quality of your soil. Mulch will need to be used fairly thickly if it is to be effective. A minimum of 2 to 3in is recommended.

Weedkillers

All weedkillers are potentially dangerous and should be used with great caution. Make sure you fully understand the instructions and that you have read them fully before you start. Avoid using weedkillers on a windy or frosty day. Wear protective clothing and gloves. Avoid inhaling if spraying and it is recommended to use a mask. Also, gloves will help to protect your skin from coming in contact with the weedkiller. If applying a weedkiller from a watering can always have one specially set aside for the job. Make sure that you have this one marked clearly with the word 'weedkiller'. You can also use a sprinkle bar attached to your watering can. It is essential that this is attached firmly. It will help to apply the weedkiller evenly and provide more economic coverage. When purchasing weedkillers there are different weedkillers for different jobs. For example, total weedkillers kill everything they come in contact with. There are also selective weedkillers such as lawn weedkillers, which are designed to kill weeds in the lawn and not the grass itself. There are several other types of weedkiller, available, ones suitable for driveways, paths and gravelled areas, which may kill and prevent weed seed germination. Always seek advice from a professional when in doubt about selecting the correct weedkiller, for a particular job. You can never be too cautious. Weedkillers and other garden chemicals must be kept out of the reach of children. If it is necessary to store a weedkiller place it in a cool, dry place and, if possible, lock it away.

Convolvulus (Bindweed)

Common Weeds

Bindweed *(Convolvulus arvensis)*
Develops a large network of fragile and brittle roots which can be left behind after digging to sprout again. Constant perseverance and the use of weedkiller is needed.

Creeping Buttercup *(Ranunculus repens)*
Travelling weed which roots quite deeply. Dig up or use weedkiller.

Scutch Grass *(Elymus repens)*
Spreading underground roots which are best dug out and carefully removed.

Mind Your Own Business *(Helexine)*
It will be necessary to use a systemic weedkiller. A persistent weed, the smallest piece left behind can regenerate into a new colony so constant attention is required to eradicate.

Creeping Buttercup

Stinging Nettle

Dandelion Seedhead

Thistle

Dandelion *(Taraxacum officinale)*

A very well-known weed which produces large tap roots. The best way to deal with this is to dig it out completely.

Stinging Nettle *(Urtica dioica)*

Small clumps are beneficial to butterflies, but where necessary dig out or use systemic weedkiller.

Thistle *(Cirsium arvense)*

Has a brittle creeping root. Hoe constantly or use mulches or weedkillers.

Chickweed *(Stellaria media)*

Continuously flowering and seeding you can use a hoe in hot weather and it can be pulled out by hand.

Helexine

Clover

Daisy

Ground Elder *(Aegopodium podagraria)*

This can be a real nuisance, not unlike bindweed. You may need to use a plastic mulch. Constant hoeing and digging will weaken. You may need to resort to a weedkiller.

Lawn Weeds

Daisy *(Bellis perennis)*

Possibly the best known of all lawn weeds. Can be removed by hand weeding or a selective lawn weedkiller.

Clover *(Trifolium)*

One of the most common lawn weeds. When in flower it is extremely popular with bumblebees. Proprietary lawn weedkiller may need to be used several times where there is a bad infestation.

Speedwell *(Veronica filiformis)*

Low, spreading, matt-forming weed with small kidney-shaped leaves and four-petalled blue flowers on very fine thread-like stalks. Can be very persistent and several selective lawn weedkiller applications may be required to control this weed.

Dandelion Leaves

Hints

Spraying Chemicals
Never spray any garden chemical during windy weather.

Watering Cans
If you have a watering can which you use for applying weedkiller it should be clearly marked and not used for anything else.

Controlling Annual Weeds
The two most useful ways for controlling annual weeds are the use of an organic mulch in layers of at least 2 to 3in deep and to use a hoe.

Applying Weedkiller
When applying a weedkiller through growing plants from a watering can use a sprinkle bar. Tape the sprinkle bar on so there is no chance of it becoming dislodged. If it were to drop off you could destroy valuable plants without meaning to.

Bindweed
If bindweed is winding its way through a hedge or other valuable plants it cannot be sprayed with a weedkiller. It may be necessary to untwine a few of the shoots. Do this carefully, making sure not to damage them. Lay these on the ground, if possible over a plastic sheet, and apply a systemic weedkiller. This will work its way through the foliage down into the root system dealing with the problem.

Scutch Grass
Never compost the roots of scutch grass as it is not always broken down or destroyed. You may find you are spreading the problem to other parts of the garden.

Dandelions
Take great care when digging out dandelions as they can regenerate from any part of the root which is left behind.

Read the Instructions
Before using a weedkiller, make sure that you have read the instructions fully. Different weedkillers do different jobs so it is important you know what you are using and how to use it correctly.

Storage
Always store weedkillers and garden chemicals out of the reach of children. Keep them in a cool, dry, safe place and always keep in original packaging. Never store in lemonade bottles, for example.

Imperial/Metric Conversion Table

DISCLAIMER: Conversions only approximate

Temperature

°F	°C
7	45
50	10
55	13
16	60
18	65
21	70

Length

in	cm
¼	0.5
½	1.0
1	2.5
12	30
24	60

Weight

oz/sq yd	g/m2	oz	g
1	35	1	28
2	70	4	113
3	100	16 (1 lb)	454
4	140	36 (2¼lb)	1000 (1 kg)

Area

sq yd	m2
1	0.8361
1¼	1.0

Volume

pints	litres
½	0.3
1¼	0.6
1¾	1.0

Conversion Formulae

To Convert	Multiply by
Inches to Centimetres	2.54
Centimetres to Inches	0.3937
Feet to Metres	0.3048
Metres to Feet	3.2808
Yards to Metres	0.9144
Metres to Yards	1.09361
Sq Inches to Sq Centimetres	6.4516
Sq Centimetres to Sq Inches	0.155
Sq Metres to Sq Feet	10.7639
Sq Feet to Sq Metres	0.092903
Sq Yards to Sq Metres	0.83613
Sq Metres to Sq Yards	1.19599
Acres to Hectares	0.40469
Hectares to Acres	2.47105
Gallons to Litres	4.546
Pounds to Grams	453.592
Grams to Pounds	0.0022

CL301013